External Linkages and Growth in Small Economies

External Linkages and Growth in Small Economies

Edited by
David L. McKee

Westport, Connecticut
London

Library of Congress Cataloging-in-Publication Data

External linkages and growth in small economies / edited by David L.
McKee.
    p. cm.
    Includes bibliographical references and index.
    ISBN 0-275-94655-X (alk. paper)
    1. Developing countries—Economic conditions. 2. Developing
countries—Economic policy. 3. Developing countries—Foreign
economic relations. 4. States, Small—Economic conditions.
5. States, Small—Foreign economic relations. I. McKee, David L.
HC59.7.E98 1994
338.9'009172'4—dc20   93-25059

British Library Cataloguing in Publication Data is available.

Library of Congress Catalog Card Number: 93-25059
ISBN: 0-275-94655-X

First published in 1994

Praeger Publishers, 88 Post Road West, Westport, CT 06881
An imprint of Greenwood Publishing Group, Inc.

Printed in the United States of America

The paper used in this book complies with the
Permanent Paper Standard issued by the National
Information Standards Organization (Z39.48-1984).

10 9 8 7 6 5 4 3 2 1

CONTENTS

TABLES

PREFACE

Earlier versions of many of the contributions to this volume were refined through presentation as papers at recent professional or academic conferences. All have resulted from original investigations by their authors and none have been previously published.

The project could not have been completed without the editorial abilities of Linda Poje, who saw it through various drafts and literally molded it into shape. Thanks are also due to James Ice of the Greenwood Publishing Group for his understanding and support.

I

A PRELIMINARY OVERVIEW

1

THE GENERAL PARAMETERS

David L. McKee

In a practical sense the advances in transportation and communications which have occurred in the second half of the twentieth century have made the world a much smaller place. With respect to business interests they have supported the emergence of a global economy. By its very existence that economy has generated irreversible alterations in the nature and positioning of production facilities and in doing that has altered the economic fortunes of nations and other political jurisdictions throughout the world. Even the strongest nations on the world scene have seen increasing threats to their economic sovereignty through the incursions of foreign interests, not to mention the actions of their own corporate players.

This new international climate brings with it both risks and opportunities for individual players, be they public or private. Multinational corporations are now able to position their production units to avail themselves of less expensive factor inputs, notably labor. Those same corporate players can also seek out locations with more permissive environmental controls and less onerous tax burdens. Such choices would be much less practical in the absence of transportation and communications improvements alluded to above.

Corporate incursions have emerged as one of the more visible ways in which Third World jurisdictions are becoming more closely linked to the global economy. Opportunities to host corporate endeavors are tempting to jurisdictions seeking ways to stimulate their economies. Of course it is the responsibility of the jurisdictions concerned to weigh the costs and benefits associated with hosting particular corporate units. Such jurisdictions will generally have the ability to reject proposed facilities which appear to be at odds with their economic needs.

The hosting of corporate facilities is evidence of increasing linkages between Third World nations and the global economy. However, the emergence of an international economy has impacted Third World jurisdictions in numerous other ways. Generally speaking, international linkages and economic sovereignty on the part of specific jurisdictions are inversely related. The more a part of the world economy a nation becomes, the less control it may have over the direction of its domestic economy.

Losing control of the domestic economy may be of special concern in small Third World nations. Today there are as many as 80 Third World jurisdictions with populations in the 10-million range or below. Although many of those nations benefit from the improved international linkages that have emerged, there may be a downside to these new circumstances as well. Because of their size smaller economies may be in a relatively weak position in dealing with the world at large. Despite that, their involvement may be proportionately much greater than that of other nations. Indeed their size may give them little choice but to become involved.

Involvement comes with the need to import goods and services from abroad. Many smaller nations lack the domestic market size to produce goods which are nonetheless needed. The only alternative is to import such products. Importing them requires that their suppliers be paid. In other words, the need for imports in turn necessitates exports. Once imports and exports are in place small economies are impacted by the movement of prices, not to mention other economic adjustments beyond their boundaries. Depending upon the magnitude of external adjustments, small economies may have to make dramatic changes in domestic priorities in order to ensure an ongoing flow of needed imports.

Any form of international involvement will impact the nature and direction of the economy in question. Hence, it is becoming clear that small Third World nations have few alternatives available which will strengthen their economies without involving them in the global picture, and it is important that policymakers in such jurisdictions inform themselves on the comparative implications of the changing menu of involvements that may be possible. In jurisdictions where policymakers have the luxury of alternatives to choose from it is hoped that the present volume will provide a better understanding of selected forms of international involvement and their implications for domestic economies.

Following this brief introduction, Yosra A. Amara provides a theoretical overview of the roles that externally traded services can play in the development of small economies. Her perspective is significant, since services have often been considered as less significant than primary and secondary pursuits in the processes of growth and development. If Amara is correct some policymakers may benefit from adjustments in their priorities.

Certainly no single volume could hope to review the advantages and disadvantages of the entire selection of international linkage options that are available in theory to small Third World nations. Similarly no single volume could assess the potential that such options hold for each and every jurisdiction contemplating their use. It is hoped that the selected insights presented here will enhance the understanding of policymakers in small Third World nations.

Part II focuses on the Caribbean. The many small nations of that region enjoy advantages over various others because of their proximity to the major markets of the North American continent. Such advantages should make the Caribbean a useful laboratory for studying the real or potential impacts of various forms of international linkage. Of course space constraints have imposed selectivity on the subjects chosen for discussion. In the first selection involving the Caribbean, Amara assesses the role of services in the growth of various small economies in the region. Following her contribution Ransford W. Palmer employs data for Jamaica to discuss how the instability of exports impacts growth in a small open economy.

In a somewhat different vein, Charles M. Byles raises the question as to whether or not Caribbean firms can compete globally. In addressing his own question Byles is concerned about the type of management style that local firms bring to bear. Certainly local firms wishing to compete internationally may have to adjust operating procedures which have supported survival if not opulence in local markets. In the final selection in Part II, Amara and McKee present an appraisal of the prospects of the Haitian economy abstracting from that nation's current political difficulties.

Part III presents some insights into real and potential impacts from international tourism in smaller economies. Many such jurisdictions have adopted that industry as a major component of their development efforts. Since many of the strengths and weaknesses of the industry in Third World settings are well understood by development specialists the focus here is both selective and specific. Mary Fish and William Gunther address issues related to political crises and international violence as they impact small island economies. These observations may be relevant in other small economies as well. The other two selections in Part III provide some insights concerning the impact of cruise ships in the Third World. In the first of those, Abbas Mamoozadeh and David L. McKee review the conflicting goals and aspirations of the cruise companies and host locations. Following that analysis the same authors shift their focus to the impact of cruise tourism in a selection of small Caribbean economies.

In Part IV the emphasis switches to specific foreign linkages as they pertain to the growth and welfare of small economies. In her final contribution to this volume, Yosra A. Amara discusses how the United States dollar impacts the small economies of the Caribbean. Following that, Palmer reviews migration from the Caribbean in a global economy.

It is hoped that the selections in this volume will provide useful insights into the various ways in which small Third World economies are becoming linked to external force fields. Although such linkages may never be risk free, it appears as though a certain amount of foreign involvement is necessary on the part of small emerging nations seeking paths to development. With this in mind the selections in this volume are offered as background to those concerned about how small Third World nations relate to the world economy.

2

EXTERNALLY TRADED SERVICES AND THE DEVELOPMENT OF SMALL ECONOMIES

Yosra A. Amara

Little awareness of the role of the service sector in small developing countries exists. Services are thought to be a developed-country issue and manufacturing is the key to economic growth. According to the theory of international trade this would be true because we assume that there are no trade barriers, whether tariff or nontariff, technology transfer, factor mobility, or differences between domestic and international trade. Under those circumstances, small economies should be able to reap all scale economies as easily as large economies. Unfortunately, real life is far from the theory of international trade, and small countries, except in special cases, find it difficult to compete in manufactured goods in the world markets.

Historically, the prices of primary commodities have declined relative to manufactured goods. For developing countries as exporters of the former and importers of the latter, export prices declined relative to import prices. Therefore, their terms of trade tended to deteriorate over time.

International trade plays a more important role in small countries' economies than in larger ones. This is because exports constitute a small proportion of outputs in most industries in large countries while the opposite is true for the small ones. Countries which are small in population and national output do not have the range of industries to provide the services of engineering and design which aid the development of internationally marketable commodities.

Economists suggest that the precise advantage of smallness lies in the ability of small countries to specialize exclusively in the production of one or few commodities in which they have comparative advantage (Jalan, 1982). However, dependence on primary commodities for export has its drawbacks, it increases the instability of returns from exports, and it is very difficult to adapt quickly to changing events. For example, when the country is producing a commodity that has large fixed costs, such as in the case of oil-producing countries, changes in the external environment such as a drop in oil prices will have immediate negative impacts.

For virtually all small countries, the prices of the commodities they trade are determined on world markets which are not affected by the quantities they trade. They are dependent economies in the sense of being price-takers. Over an interval of time the prices of their export commodities relative to the price of the bundle of commodities they import will change. When relative prices change permanently, the relative profitability of producing different goods also changes, and this induces producers to increase the quantities produced of commodities which have become more profitable, ignoring the comparative advantage issue.

The limited production possibilities of small countries reduce the ability of the economy to adjust to shocks which have reduced the profitability of the leading sectors. Hence, small developing countries' exports are, by far, determined by the economic activities of industrialized countries, such as commodity composition and commodity prices (*World Development Report*, 1988).

Some large developing countries, such as Korea, Brazil, Taiwan, and Thailand have opted to develop modern industrial sectors to serve the domestic and the international markets. This has been done by introducing import substitution and export-oriented goods. The techniques of production are invented in developed countries where unskilled labor is relatively expensive. Most developed countries are reasonably large in population and income. Therefore, those techniques tend to embody an optimal scale of operation which is large enough to meet industries' demand, but too large relative to the capacity of markets available to small developing countries since they are small in population and income. This is not to suggest that economies of scale are a function of population or country size, but rather a function of the scale of output. Therefore, the extent to which a country can exploit such economies of scale in any industry depends on the extent of the market. The extent of the domestic market depends on the size of the population and the level of per capita income.

Thereupon, a small country may not be able to sustain an international competitive position because it cannot exploit economies of scale as fully as large countries, and its domestic market is unlikely to grow rapidly due to continuous adverse terms of trade effects. Then, industrialization cannot be geared to the home markets because of their small size. As such, the only feasible development strategy in small countries with limited natural resources lies in the creation of export-oriented industries or services. However, because manufacturing is usually more capital intensive than most other activities (e.g., farming, banking, tourism), economies of scale and factor indivisibilities tend to be more important. It follows that countries with small domestic markets caused by small populations as well as income are generally at a disadvantage, compared with larger countries, in undertaking manufacturing activities. Hence, the existing international trade system disfavors the small developing countries and virtually guarantees an export market for the major industrial countries' manufactured goods with their high degree of value added, and it will be very difficult for the small developing countries to break the barriers to sustained economic growth. It has been pointed out by Lloyd and Sundrum that small population means that human resources and skills are likely to be scarce, and facilities for the development of human resources may be highly limited compared with larger countries. The small size of population and the alternative demand for skilled manpower may constitute an important constraint on development potential (Lloyd and Sundrum, 1982). When manufacturing and the exploitation of natural resources are not adequate to balance import requirements, greater specialization in the export of services might bring an economic revival. This is not to say that economies can escape being involved in the three sectors.

Currently, the role of agriculture in small developing countries is declining due to the continuous decline in prime commodity prices. At the same time, those countries cannot develop a heavy manufacturing sector due to the smallness of their local market and due to the lack of capital and technology. Thus, neither primary nor secondary sector's exports could provide the market share needed to generate employment and foreign exchange.

Under these circumstances it is likely that only sectors, like services, that are not generally subject to increasing returns to scale can provide a long-term escape route for small developing countries which have limited resources. Amit Bhaduri et al. (1982) showed that the services sector in a small economy has neither the disadvantage of the industrial sector dominated by the scale effect nor the limitation of given land-man ratios which characterize the labor productivity of agriculture.

While it should be clear that, by and large, the service sector is less sophisticated in small developing countries than in industrial ones, developing countries are certainly capable of replicating some services. Small developing countries can have some sources of comparative advantage in the production of services, such as geographical location and natural endowments which can be exploited in both transportation and tourism services. Therefore, small developing countries export mainly consumer services such as travel and tourism, while developed countries export producer services, areas that involve advanced technology. Moreover, services can be produced in small developing countries to meet the international demand well before the local market demands those services.

Agriculture and manufacturing will continue to be important, but services will facilitate the mobility of goods, information, and labor. Mass production and increased returns to scale in manufactured goods were made possible only because services could link markets and establishments through improved distribution channels, thus extending the markets. The extension of the markets starts a chain reaction. It makes specialization possible due to economies of scale, hence the development of new markets. In other words, extending markets for certain services contributes to the extension of markets for industrial goods. In many cases the development of the service sector is not a result of growth, rather, it is one of its conditions. All functioning economies require a productive interplay among agriculture, manufacturing, and services, and all economies must have functional service sectors.

However, services assume special and important roles in small developing countries because they provide essential links among economic agents. It is necessary to notice that some countries rely on service surpluses to offset the deficits in their balance of payments. Services are strongly linked with the rest of the economy due to their role in the production of goods. Therefore, trade in services is important at all levels of development. Nonetheless, it is possible to find differences in the rate of growth of services between two countries with equal real incomes.

The service sector in a small economy has neither the disadvantage of the industrial sector dominated by the scale effect nor the limitation of given land-man ratios which characterize the labor productivity of agriculture. A higher level of technology has resulted in a direct shift in economic structure from agriculture to services.

The pressing need for developing countries to accelerate the growth of their exports is based on two major purposes: to generate employment and to earn the foreign exchange needed to pay for their imports and to service foreign loans. Since neither primary nor secondary exports could provide the market share needed to sustain these objectives, it is important to consider service sectors as tools for economic growth in small developing countries.

Economists have suggested that the importance of services increases with economic growth (Fuchs, 1968; McKee, 1988 and 1991; Nell, 1988). They consider rising income, urbanization, and industrialization the most influential factors that increase the importance of services. Hence, services may not be expected to play a major role in developing countries' economies, they may be considered the result, rather than the cause of growth.

Allan G. B. Fisher (1939) divided economic activities into primary, secondary, and tertiary activities. The assumption is that as countries develop, they transfer employment and activities from the agricultural sector to the industrial sector and then to the service sector. The increase in per capita income and the growth of cities demand that services should grow for the same reason that other industries have grown. As population becomes more urban, it has been almost inevitable that more banks, more schools, and more of various other services are needed. Moreover, Katouzian (1970) argued that the rise in per capita income in industrialized countries will affect the growth of services in small developing countries. As the level of income grows, the demand for recreation in developing countries will push small developing countries toward offering recreational services such as travel and tourism. This in turn will raise per capita income in small developing countries and the demand for services will expand. Therefore, certain services in developing countries were provided in response to the needs of foreign interests from developed countries. Producer services were, to some extent, an effect of the internationalization of production, which in turn occurred with the expansion of multinational corporations in the 1960s. For multinational corporations to operate in a developing country, there should be a healthy and literate work force, administrative and management skills, marketing, legal and accounting services, a well-developed financial market, as well as advanced transportation, communications, and construction service sectors. However, some large developing countries could establish a service sector that is not a response to industrialized countries' demand. Ronald Shelp (1981) noted that the success of Brazil, Korea, and other developing countries in winning major construction contracts in both developing and industrial countries is not a result of foreign demand, but rather an indication that developing countries can successfully creat international service industries.

Although Fisher's division of economic growth implies that an economy should pass through three stages of development, this view also implies that there is an integration within sectors as the service content of each increases. From the point of view of small developing countries, this is critically important, because it implies a close link between service and nonservice activities. In other words, services are strongly linked with the rest of the economy and they play a critical role in the production of goods. Hence, services are both causes and effects of economic growth, and their importance to developing countries cannot be ignored.

Conventional wisdom has assumed that the key to development lies in industrialization by using labor intensive technology. This argument ignores the integration within sectors. Services are becoming more intertwined with goods. The service sector is a vital force in stimulating and facilitating economic growth. All economies are dependent on the development of appropriate public administration structures and financial markets in order for economic activities to take place. Dorothy Riddle (1987) suggested that the Industrial Revolution itself was dependent on changes in the service sector. Development of factories was only possible because of the growth of capital markets. Mass production was dependent upon the development of transportation that allowed the timely arrival of raw materials and finished goods, management skills and technological advancement, and the availability of large markets that developed through international trade. Goods and services are interdependent and mutually supportive. The role of services such as transportation, and utilities in general, are a crucial part of a country's infrastructure.

The role of services in terms of employment, percentage of GDP, and international involvement is extremely important for developing countries (most developing countries are small). In 1981, an average of 18 percent of the labor force was engaged in services in those countries.[1] This figure was 59 percent for Singapore, 30 percent for Indonesia, 34 percent for Malaysia, and 37 percent for the Philippines. The increase of the service share in employment has been accompanied by an increase in their share in GDP. For the year 1987 the services' share was about 31.4 percent of GDP, taken as an average, for all developing countries. In 32 developing countries, services originated half or more than half of GDP. Among them 5 countries were classified as low-income economies, 19 were considered to be middle-income economies, and 8 were upper-middle-income economies. Thirty-nine developing countries were net exporters of services and have shown surpluses in their services' trade in the year 1987.

According to the *World Development Report* (World Bank, 1989), the average growth rate of service exports for the period 1980 to 1987 was 5.1 percent for the low-income economies. The same rate was 3.1 percent for the middle-income economies. The comparison shows that developing countries have experienced higher service-growth rates than industrialized countries.

Small developing countries constitute a small market compared to world trade, in any incoming or outgoing commodity, meaning that they are price-takers. Small developing countries need to earn the foreign exchange required to pay for their imports and to service their foreign loans. Since aid by trade is the engine to trigger their development, their close integration with the world economy and their orientation toward world markets is expected to trigger and maintain the development process. Their exposure to foreign trade is such that economic targets are often beyond their control. Therefore, their capacity to earn foreign exchange is highly dependent on their ability to gain access to world markets. Free access to the markets of developed countries and the elimination of any impediment to trade are of crucial importance. If trade barriers such as those of technology transfer and factor mobility can be overcome, small developing countries can establish a trading pattern which will have different characteristics from those of large developed countries. Small economies can have a comparative advantage in the production and export of products which are amenable to relatively small-scale production and less capital intensive either in goods or services.

All functioning economies require a productive interplay among the three economic sectors, agriculture, manufacturing, and services. In addition, physical infrastructure must be developed in each economy in order to support other productive activities. Transportation and communications are essential to the functioning of any economy. Social infrastructure development (health, education, public administration) is also crucial in providing a competent work force and an environment in which productive activities can flourish. When the manufacturing sector and the exploitation of natural resources are not adequate to balance import requirements, greater specialization in the export of services might lead to economic revival. However, the capital available to those countries, their technological capabilities (access to technology), and the skill level of their labor force should guarantee them a comparative advantage in the marketing of these services.

Technological advancements made it possible for the small economies to shift directly from agriculture to services, in a sense that the growth of both manufacturing and services can occur concomitantly. The computer and its data and other processing functions have revolutionized productivity trends in the service industries. Moreover, the declining cost of microelectronic products has made the use of data banks and advanced communications more accessible to small countries. It is the rapid growth of the service sector that makes the difference between the high- and the low-growth countries. As the service sector becomes more dependent on information technology, a literate and skilled work force becomes a definite asset. Language capabilities can also constitute a comparative advantage. For example, both Jamaica and Barbados are promoting their skilled literate, English-speaking population.

International trade in services in small developing countries continues to flourish. The reason is that many services are relatively cheaper in small developing economies than in large industrial ones. The real price of services relative to goods tends to rise with higher levels of per capita income. This suggests that small developing countries have a comparative advantage in the provision of labor-intensive services. For this reason an increasing number of data processing companies have found the Caribbean countries to be attractive. Caribbean countries where data entry employees earn considerably less than their United States counterparts have become the centers for United States "offshore office" operations. Although this comparative advantage may be eroded, the "offshore office" operations offer an economic revival mainly through generating foreign exchange.

Services can help in solving the problems that small developing countries are facing due to the constraints imposed by size for development of a manufacturing sector. Moreover, services can also help agriculture to flourish and therefore increase its contribution to economic development.

It appears that there are reasons for the importance of service credits in foreign exchange earnings of small developing countries. They have a comparative advantage in trade in services, as compared to the production of goods for export. This is mainly due to the low cost of labor force and to the lesser importance of economies of scale in providing a number of services. At the same time, technical progress has fostered some decentralization of numerous service activities, such as data services, by making them more economical, which could work in favor of small developing countries. Since data are still entered in computers by manual typing, low labor costs in the developing countries give them a comparative advantage in such pursuits. In fact, some U.S. corporations have transferred a share of this most labor-intensive phase of data processing abroad.

Although service industries are important for economic development, without growing foreign demand for services, small developing countries will be hard-pressed to sustain high growth over a long period of time. Consequently, the role that the service sector can play in the long-run growth process of a small country is contingent upon the foreign demand for those services. There remains a considerable amount of work to be done in this area. In particular, more work is needed to derive a set of estimates for the demand for and the supply of exports of services from small developing countries. This would add to our knowledge of how countries can use policies to change the mix of their exports and thereby improve their external positions. If small countries wish to improve their long-run growth prospects, they need to capture a good export share in world markets. This means that there is a need to identify those services for which there is a demand overseas. Moreover, the choice of export activities poses the question of the extent to which it is desirable to diversify exports in terms of both products and markets. More diversification would tend to shield the economy from price and quantity fluctuations, but this has to be balanced against the economies of scale in production, acquisition of technology, and overseas marketing.

NOTE

1.   The figures in this paragraph were derived from information contained in the *World Development Report*, 1989.

II

SOME SPECIFICS FROM THE CARIBBEAN

3

SERVICES AND GROWTH IN SMALL DEVELOPING COUNTRIES

Yosra A. Amara

In many small developing countries neither agriculture nor manufacturing alone appear able to generate growth. The effects of service industries on economic growth have not been given adequate consideration. Services are industries that play a vital and dynamic role in any functioning economy in a sense that they stimulate growth in other sectors. Services assume special importance for developing countries because they provide essential links among economic agents. When manufacturing and the exploitation of natural resources are not adequate to balance import requirements, greater specialization in the export of services might bring an economic revival.

This chapter will investigate the possibility of the service sector as a tool for economic growth in small developing countries. The first part of the chapter will try to investigate the importance of each of the three sectors to economic growth through its contribution to the growth of gross domestic product. The second part will try to identify those individual services, the development of which would be beneficial for economic growth in those small developing countries.

THE IMPORTANCE OF SERVICE SECTORS TO SMALL ECONOMIES

Economists suggest that the precise advantage of smallness lies in the ability of small countries to specialize exclusively in the production of one or few commodities in which they have comparative advantage (Jalan, 1982). However, dependence on primary commodities for export has its drawbacks. It increases the instability of returns from exports, and it is very difficult to adapt quickly to changing events. For virtually all small countries, the prices of the commodities they trade are determined on world markets which are not affected by the quantities they trade. They are dependent economies in the sense of being price-takers. The prices of their export commodities relative to the price of the bundle of commodities they import are changing. Since relative price changes are not in their favor, producers are expected to increase the quantities produced of commodities which have become more profitable, ignoring the comparative advantage principle. The limited production possibilities of small countries reduce the ability of the economy to adjust to shocks which have reduced the profitability of the leading sectors. Hence, small developing countries' exports are, by far, determined by the economic activities of industrial countries such as commodity composition and commodity prices. Moreover, trade policies in industrial countries influence the options available for developing countries' exports. For example, agricultural products in some industrial countries are becoming highly protected and subsidized. In certain products, developing countries are prevented from expanding into traditional industrial country markets. Therefore, trade in commodity exports is declining in relative importance for developing countries.

In manufacturing industries, the techniques of production are invented in developed countries where unskilled labor is relatively expensive and most developed countries are reasonably large. Therefore, those techniques tend to embody an optimal scale of operation which is large enough to meet industrial countries' demand, but too large relative to the capacity of markets available to developing countries since most developing countries are small in population and income. Thereupon, a small country may not be able to sustain an international competitive position because it cannot exploit economies of scale as fully as a large country, and its domestic market is unlikely to grow rapidly due to continuous adverse terms of trade effects. Then, industrialization cannot be geared to the home market because of its small size. As such, the only feasible development strategy in small countries with limited natural resources lies in the creation of export-oriented industries and services.

SELECTION OF THE COUNTRIES

For the present investigation the following countries from the Eastern Caribbean have been selected: Antigua and Barbuda, Barbados, St. Lucia, St. Kitts-Nevis, and St. Vincent and the Grenadines. The decision to select those countries was guided by several considerations. They are all small, and smallness means that economic growth must inevitably be export-oriented. Other than in exceptional circumstances, rapid growth requires strong competitiveness in commodity or service exports. All the countries chosen are similar in the openness of their economies. They all have small resource bases, and depend heavily on a narrow range of export goods together with agricultural products and tourism. Services may well play major roles in the economic growth of those countries. Indeed those countries may have comparative advantages in the production of services due to their proximity to North America, their literate labor force, relative political stability, and good infrastructure. Certain services can be developed in those countries in response to needs of foreign interests from developed countries (North America and Europe).

A MODEL OF SERVICES

While a model of service-based economic growth has not been constructed, the models that are presented in the economic literature treat services either on an aggregate level or take one variable at a time. Some of these models have treated developing countries in the same way that they treated developed countries (Gemmell, 1982). While the assumptions under which the model can be applied to developed countries are valid, these assumptions are not necessarily valid when applying the same model to developing countries. Hence, the first part of the model in this chapter will try to investigate the contribution of each of the three sectors to economic growth. The second part will try to examine the service sector in order to identify those individual services, the development of which would be beneficial for economic growth in small developing countries. There are many services such as banking, insurance, recreation, and tourism that can develop simultaneously with various manufacturing industries, and the growth of these services would stimulate economic growth.

Assumptions

The model for this study will be developed within certain procedural parameters. First, in this model, the intention is not to predict, or to determine the value of the dependent variable, or to produce the best fitted model. Rather, the purpose is to project the contribution of each of the sectors or the individual service to the growth of gross domestic product. For example, which sector/ service contributes the most to the growth of gross domestic product. Second, no attempt will be made to show the merits of one theoretical approach over another. Third, the main orientation of the study is empirical and the results should be statistically observable regardless of which theoretical method is used. The emphasis will be placed on the examination of the three sectors and the mix of services. On the basis of a careful differentiation of the three sectors and of the various types of services in a particular country, it may be possible to evaluate which sector or which type of service(s) should become the target of development strategy. Fourth, and most importantly, a change in one sector accompanied by a change in another sector does not imply a cause-effect relationship.

The Dependent Variable

The dependent variable that has been chosen is the growth in gross domestic product. The choice of this variable is based on the belief that it is a good indicator of economic growth. Moreover, in reviewing the literature about economic development, it was found that the universal factor of the regression equations of economic growth is usually proxied by per capita income or gross domestic product (see, for example, Clark, 1940; Kuznets, 1965; Fuchs, 1968; and Singelmann, 1978). Therefore, the following hypothesis will be tested among the countries chosen: the higher the level of value added by a sector or by an individual service, the higher the level of gross domestic product.

The Independent Variables

Data on services in small developing countries are scarcely available, and even those that are available suffer from questionable reliability. The data published by the World Bank are too aggregated to shed much light on recent developments in the service industries. Service activities are both numerous and diverse in themselves and in the changes they effect in goods and economic growth. Although it is believed that Katouzian's or Singelmann's categorization (Katouzian, 1970; and Singelmann, 1978) can produce more concrete results than the World Bank data, the latter will be used due to their availability, and to make the results comparable. Nevertheless, the decision was to exclude government and private services. It is common to do so, or to separate government and private services (see for example Kuznets, 1971; and Stigler, 1956). Therefore, quarterly data have been obtained from the World Bank for the period of the 1970s and 1980s (approximately 1976-1987). For the first part of the analysis the data include value added by agriculture, value added by manufacturing, value added by services, and gross domestic product. For the second part of the analysis, the data include value added by commerce, value added by tourism, value added by transportation and communications, value added by business services, and gross domestic product.

The Model's Equations

In testing the model, the linear form was found to give the best fit. However, some of the independent variables are correlated, and independence of variables is a prerequisite of multiple regression. Therefore, stepwise regression was used to compare the independent variables. Also some transformation was needed, and the logarithmic form gave the best results. Hence, the model's equations were as follows: Sector equations:

Log Y = B0 + B1 log X1 + B2 log X2 + B3 log X3 + E
where:

    Y   = Gross domestic product.
    X1 = Value added by agriculture.
    X2 = Value added by manufacturing.
    X3 = Value added by services.
    B0 = Constant term.
    E   = Random error term.

Individual service equations:

Log Y = B0 + B4 log X4 + B5 log X5 + B6 log X6 +
      B7 log X7 + E
where:

    X4 = Value added by commerce.
    X5 = Value added by tourism.
    X6 = Value added by transportation and communications.
    X7 = Value added by business services.

Since the response variable has been re-expressed, the predicted values are in the transformed scale. Nonetheless, it is not necessary to convert the predicted values back to the original units for two reasons. First, the objective of the study is not to construct the best fitted model that can predict the dependent variable, but rather to make comparisons among the independent variables in the model. Second, since the model is in logarithmic form, the beta coefficients represent the elasticities of the dependent variables under study. Finding the elasticities of the variables is one of the objectives of the economic model.

ANALYZING THE RESULTS

Although balance of payments statistics barely exist for many small developing countries, many of them clearly depend on invisible earnings to finance their imports. In 1987 four out of the five countries involved in this study have shown the item "service credits" to be greater than the item "merchandise exports." These figures are 548 percent, 442 percent, 229 percent, 114.30 percent, and 30.50 percent for Antigua and Barbuda, Barbados, St. Lucia, St. Kitts-Nevis, and St. Vincent and the Grenadines respectively (World Bank, 1988).

Antigua and Barbuda

Table 3.1 shows the stepwise regression results for Antigua's and Barbuda's data. Services is the strongest variable that affects growth of gross domestic product with an R^2 of 0.94 and an elasticity of 1.11. Agriculture seems to be the second most influential variable, followed by manufacturing. Corresponding R^2s are shown to be 0.16 and 0.01 respectively.

With respect to the comparison among the four types of services, Table 3.2 presents the results for the countries under study. For Antigua and Barbuda, the variable business services has the highest association with gross domestic product with an R^2 of 0.98 and elasticity of 1.20. Commerce shows a somewhat weak relationship with gross domestic product, R^2 is 0.02 and the elasticity is 0.80.

Barbados

For Barbados, Table 3.1 shows that the services variable is the one directly responsible for growth of gross domestic product. The association is a strong one with an R^2 of 0.96 and elasticity of 0.79. Manufacturing contributes another 0.01 to R^2 and an elasticity of 0.12. Agriculture does not show any significance with regard to the contribution to the growth of gross domestic product.

In Table 3.2, the comparison between the four types of services shows that the strongest explanatory variable of economic growth in Barbados is commerce followed by tourism, business services, and transportation and communications. R^2s were shown to be 0.92, 0.03, 0.01, and 0.004 respectively.

Table 3.1
The Influence of the Three Sectors on Gross Domestic Product

Country	Sector	B Value	R**2	F Value	Prob> F
Antigua	Agriculture	0.35	0.02	15.90	0.0006
& Barbuda	Manufacturing	0.23	0.01	4.82	0.0379
	Services	1.11	0.94	167.86	0.0001
Barbados	Agriculture				
	Manufacturing	0.12	0.01	7.86	0.0074
	Services	0.79	0.96	1195.00	0.0001
St. Kitts-	Agriculture				
Nevis	Manufacturing				
	Services	0.47	0.97	882.89	0.0001
St. Lucia	Agriculture				
	Manufacturing	0.16	0.02	20.31	0.0001
	Services	0.65	0.95	469.78	0.0001
St. Vincent	Agriculture	0.12	0.01	24.16	0.0001
& the	Manufacturing	0.13	0.01	40.33	0.0001
Grenadines	Services	0.76	0.98	240.06	0.0001

Note: All variables in the table are significant at the 5 % level.

Table 3.2
The Influence of Individual Service Variables
on the Gross Domestic Product

Country	Service	B Value	R**2	FValue	Prob>F
Antigua & Barbuda	Commerce	0.84	0.02	80.04	0.0001
	Tourism				
	Transport				
	Business	1.18	0.98	75.67	0.0001
Barbados	Commerce	0.38	0.92	26.55	0.0001
	Tourism	0.16	0.03	53.44	0.0001
	Transport	0.01	0.004	5.34	0.0257
	Business	0.21	0.008	8.81	0.0030
St. Kitts-Nevis	Commerce				
	Tourism	0.03	0.002	15.51	0.0005
	Transport	0.17	0.02	173.98	0.0001
	Business	0.61	0.97	152.93	0.0001
St. Lucia	Commerce	0.50	0.01	11.07	0.0019
	Tourism				
	Transport	0.27	0.87	13.59	0.0001
	Business	0.42	0.06	44.87	0.0001
St. Vincent & the Grenadines	Commerce				
	Tourism	0.27	0.01	10.47	0.0026
	Transport	0.17	0.01	12.96	0.0020
	Business	0.82	0.96	15.42	0.0001

Note: All variables in the table are significant at the 5 % level.

St. Kitts-Nevis

From Table 3.1 it can be seen that services show the strongest link with gross domestic product with an R^2 of 0.97 and an elasticity of 0.47. The other two variables do not show any significant association with gross domestic product.

From Table 3.1 it is evident that the variable that is directly responsible for the growth of gross domestic product is business services with an R^2 of 0.97 and an elasticity of 0.62. The transportation and communications variable is the second most influential, followed by tourism with R^2s of 0.02, 0.002, and elasticities of 0.17, and 0.03 respectively.

St. Lucia

In St. Lucia services show the strongest association with gross domestic product where the R^2 is shown to be 0.95 and the elasticity is 0.65. Manufacturing seems to be the second most important variable with respect to its contribution to the growth of gross domestic product. The R^2 is 0.02 and the elasticity is 0.16. Agriculture does not seem to make a significant contribution to the growth of gross domestic product (see Table 3.1).

Table 3.2 shows that the transportation and communications variable has the strongest influence on gross domestic product with an R^2 of 0.92 and an elasticity of 0.27. The business services variable contributes another 0.06 to R^2 and has an elasticity of 0.43. Commerce has contributed another 0.01 to the R^2 with an elasticity of 0.50.

St. Vincent and the Grenadines

The services variable shows the highest contribution to gross domestic product with an R^2 of 0.98 and an elasticity of 0.76 while manufacturing and agriculture contribute another 0.01 each to the R^2 with elasticities of 0.13 and 0.12 respectively (see Table 3.1).

Table 3.2 shows that the variable that has the strongest association with gross domestic product is business services with an R^2 of 0.96 and an elasticity of 0.82. The variables transportation and communications, and tourism show a contribution to R^2 of 0.01 each and elasticities of 0.17 and 0.27 respectively.

CONCLUDING REMARKS

The role of the service sector in the economies of the Caribbean countries under study is more prominent and central than is commonly believed. Services explained large portions of the variability in economic performance for all of the countries under study. The value added by services is strongly associated with economic growth proxied by gross domestic product. Exporting of services deserves as much concern by policymakers as does the exporting of merchandise.

The results suggest a positive association between services and economic growth. Economic development strategies need to place more emphasis on service sector development. While all sectors are important for any economy, service sector development seems to be crucial for those countries' economic growth. In order for progress to be made, it is essential that countries should be able to identify areas of clear importance so that they have a stake in the outcome.

Small Caribbean nations, like other countries, would be wise to develop on the basis of the assets they have. Although it is difficult to establish general appropriate economic policies which would be relevant to all countries in the study, the problems and the constraints are common enough to permit at least a few broad conclusions in regard to development policies. First and most important, there is a need for an appropriate allocation of resources. For Antigua and Barbuda, St. Kitts-Nevis, and St. Vincent and the Grenadines, business services should receive more attention in resource allocation strategy since they are expected to have the most positive influence on the growth of the economy. Barbados should direct more resources to commerce and St. Lucia should consider its transportation and communications sector as a significant factor that affects the growth of the economy. Second, it is important to know that, when stepwise results do not show any significance with a variable such as agriculture, it does not mean that the variable should be ignored, but rather, it is not the variable of choice for additional resource allocation. It is not a variable propelling growth for this country. If it is to play a more positive role in the economy, changes need to occur first in the supporting infrastructure activities. Indeed, when using one variable at a time in the regression run, all of the variables show strong association with gross domestic product. Economically, it has been evident from this study that the service sector plays a vital and critical role in those countries' economic growth.

4

EXPORT EARNINGS INSTABILITY AND ECONOMIC GROWTH IN JAMAICA, 1957 TO 1986

Ransford W. Palmer

INTRODUCTION

Over the thirty-year period between 1957 and 1986, Jamaica experienced some of the classic problems of export earnings instability faced by small open developing countries. This experience has made it a particularly good example for a case study of the causes and effects of that instability. Over the period, Jamaica's export earnings grew from 27.9 percent to 52.6 percent of gross domestic product, while the structure of its exports evolved from a dominance of primary commodities--mainly bauxite, alumina, and sugar--to a dominance of services--mainly tourism. During that time, the share of sugar exports fell sharply from 28 percent to less than 4 percent. The dominance of sugar was replaced by bauxite and alumina, which together reached their peak share of 58 percent by the middle of the 1970s. By the beginning of the 1980s, the dominance of bauxite and alumina gave way to services, particularly tourism, which accounted for half of all export earnings by 1986. Thus, despite the thrust of development policy toward export diversification, the evolution of exports has essentially been a substitution of services for primary commodities.

Virtually all of the studies of export instability have focused on primary commodities because of their traditional vulnerability to world market conditions. But tourism is also vulnerable, and probably even more so. It is particularly sensitive to economic conditions in the origin countries and to political developments in the destination ones.

The growth of Jamaica's tourism faltered badly in the 1970s due largely to the rise in petroleum cost and a political climate in Jamaica which discouraged tourism and private foreign investment. In the 1980s, it took off again as economic growth in the United States and Europe accelerated after the 1980-1982 recession and as the political climate in Jamaica became more accommodating to an expanded tourist industry. Thus, despite the change in the structure of export earnings, these earnings remain highly vulnerable to external conditions.

The main purpose of this chapter is to examine the sources of export earnings instability and to estimate the impact of that instability on Jamaica's economic growth over the period from 1957 to 1986. The chapter has four parts. Part one measures the instability of export earnings and the direction of that instability over the period; part two examines the sources of export earnings instability; part three estimates the impact of export growth and instability on the gross domestic product; and part four draws some conclusions.

The data used in this study were taken from the International Monetary Fund publication, International Financial Statistics, and from a number of official publications of the Government of Jamaica. All data, except where otherwise indicated, are in nominal values and have been converted into indices with 1980 as the base year.

MEASURING THE INSTABILITY OF EXPORT EARNINGS

Drawing on Massel (1964) and Lim (1983), I have chosen the ratio of the standard error of the estimate of the ordinary least squares regression of a variable on its time trend to the mean of that variable as the measure of its instability. And I have chosen the estimate of the equation form, $\log Y = a + bX$, because it provided the best fit for the data. Table 4.1 shows the estimated instability indices for the relevant variables for the thirty-year period (1957-1986) and for the sub-periods (1957-73 and 1974-86). Of the principal components of the value of exports, services (VSER) have the largest instability index (.122) and bauxite the smallest (.075) for the thirty-year period. Of all the variables in Table 4.1, the price of sugar (PSUG) was by far the most unstable (.218), followed by tourist receipts (TR) (.145).

To assess the direction of instability, I divided the thirty-year period into two sub-periods, with 1973 as the dividing line, which, as

Table 4.1
Estimated Indices of Instability[1]

Year	1957-73	1974-86	1957-86
Total Exports (TEX)	.019	.067	.077
Merchandise Exports (MEX)	.043	.053	.082
Value of Service Exports (VSER)	.106	.038	.122
Value of Alumina Exports (VALU)	.146	.063	.199
Value of Bauxite Exports (VBAX)	.082	.067	.075
Value of Sugar Exports (VSUG)	.048	.072	.082
Quantity of Alumina Exports (QALU)	.049	.034	.084
Quantity of Bauxite Exports (QBAX)	.023	.049	.071
Quantity of Sugar Exports (QSUG)	.028	.031	.040
Exchange Rate of Jamaican Dollar (EXR)	.012	.047	.085
Price of Aluminum (PALU)	.012	.056	.056
Price of Sugar (New York) (PSUG)	.201	.133	.218
Tourist Receipts (TR)	.061	.060	.145
Gross Domestic Product	.038	.017	.051
Imported Machinery and Transportation Equipment (MTE)	.063	.104	.099

1. The indices are the ratio of the standard error of the estimate of the ordinary least squares regression of the log of each variable on time to the mean of each variable.

Michael Whitter (1983) puts it, "cut(s) across the post-independence history of the Jamaican economy like a transversal separating a decade of growth from a decade of stagnation and crisis." One explanation of this dichotomy is that the external shocks of the pre-1973 period were for the most part favorable, while those of the post-1973 period were mostly unfavorable. In the pre-1973 period, commodity prices rose and the cost of air travel declined with the introduction of the more efficient jet airliners serving the Caribbean. This meant greater earnings for commodity exports and a sharp increase in the growth of tourism. Together, these developments stimulated an inflow of foreign capital which accelerated economic growth.

The oil shocks of the 1970s raised import prices while the worldwide recession of the early 1980s depressed export prices and reduced the flow of tourists. The decline of tourism was also the result of the hostile political and social climate prevailing in Jamaica during the 1970s. But even when the industry recovered in the 1980s, it was unable to offset the negative impact of the decline of commodity exports on the economy by 1986. This raises the question of whether tourism can be the engine of growth in the same way that commodities were in the 1960s. The large instability index for the value of services in Table 4.1 suggests that a tourist economy may be even more volatile than one which depends on primary commodity exports. Yet because the world demand for tourism is rising faster than the world demand for primary commodities, a rational development strategy must ensure that Jamaica shares in that growth.

The instability indices for the sub-periods 1957 to 1973 and 1974 to 1985 (Table 4.1) show that total export earnings (TEX) and merchandise export earnings (MEX) were more unstable in the second period than in the first, suggesting that the instability of the entire period (1957-86) was primarily influenced by what happened between 1973 and 1986. Yet when the value and volume of exports are disaggregated, this trend of instability does not hold for services, alumina, and bauxite. Sugar, on the other hand, exhibited an increase in instability in both value and volume over the two sub-periods. In both sub-periods, the instability of the earnings of alumina, bauxite, and sugar was greater than the instability of their volumes, a phenomenon that must be attributed to the greater instability of their prices.

While the instability of merchandise trade increased in the post-1973 period, the instability of services declined. Yet, as was indicated earlier, services had a higher instability index than merchandise exports over the entire thirty-year period. The implication is that the overall instability of services was heavily influenced by what happened before 1973: the share of services in export earnings rose sharply in the 1960s and fell equally sharply in the early 1970s. The sharpest increase in instability over the two sub-periods occurred in the exchange rate and in the price of alumina. The one was the result of several major devaluations of the Jamaican dollar, since it was revalued in 1973 and tied to the U.S. dollar, and the other the result of falling aluminum prices in the world market.

SOURCES OF EXPORT GROWTH AND INSTABILITY

David Murray, in his 1978 cross-section study, concluded that "in the majority of underdeveloped countries quantity fluctuations were consistently the dominant contributor to earnings variations." However, for some of the countries in Murray's study (which used data for 1952-1971), price fluctuations were more important than quantity fluctuations. The relevance of Murray's findings for Jamaica is uncertain, since no English-speaking Caribbean country was included in his study. Thus our examination of the Jamaican case may or may not confirm Murray's conclusions, particularly because our study covers a longer time period and uses time series analysis.

To assess the impact of quantity and price changes on the principal components of exports, I regressed the export earnings of alumina, bauxite, sugar, and tourism on their respective volumes and world prices as well as on the prevailing exchange rate.[1] In the case of tourism, tourist receipts were used as a proxy for the world price of tourism and the number of tourist arrivals as the volume. Table 4.2 shows that the most significant coefficients are tourist receipts, the exchange rate, the price of aluminum, and the price of sugar. It is reasonable to conclude, therefore, that price changes were more important than quantity changes in explaining variations in export earnings. If I accept the standard argument that the world demand for a small country's exports is highly elastic and that the supply of those exports is inelastic, then a change in the foreign price of those exports

Table 4.2
Coefficients of the Determinants of the Main Components of Export Earnings, 1957-1986

Independent Variables	Dependent Variables			
	LVALU	LVBAX	LVSUG	LVSER
Constant	-9.132	-11.165	-4.838	-2.455
	(-34.14)	(-10.79)	(-2.08)	(-1.02)
LQALU	1.040			
	(13.68)			
LPALU	1.189	.826		
	(8.43)	(5.09)		
LNOT				.657
				(1.65)
LEXR	.787	1.359	1.155	.231
	(10.01)	(9.68)	(6.95)	(.495)
LQBAX		1.261		
		(6.85)		
LQSUG			.547	
			(1.88)	
LPSUG			.386	
			(4.78)	
LTR				.657
				(1.92)
R^2 (Adjusted)	.92	.95	.87	.95
DW	2.38	2.91	2.99	1.99

The letter L in front of the variables indicates log. t statistics are in parentheses.

will be affected only by a change in the demand for them. Since such a change in demand is the result only of a change in foreign economic conditions, fluctuations in the domestic value of export earnings must be attributed to those external conditions.

The next step is to examine how each of the principal components of exports affected total export earnings. My approach here is to distinguish between their impact on the growth and their impact on the instability of total export earnings. Thus two regressions were run, one using the log form of the actual data of the variables and the other using the residuals of each variable around its time trend. Table 4.3 shows that services (mainly tourism) and alumina exports had the greatest impact on the growth of total export earnings. However, their contribution to the instability of export earnings, as shown in Table 4.4, is larger than their contribution to the growth of those earnings. This suggests that as economic growth becomes more dependent on these exports, it is likely to be characterized by a greater degree of instability.

THE IMPACT OF EXPORT EARNINGS INSTABILITY ON OUTPUT GROWTH

As in the above analysis, the procedure here is a two-step one. First, I look at the relationship between the growth of export earnings and the growth of output (GDP) and then I look at the impact of the instability of export earnings on the instability of output growth. Thus, as before, growth and instability are treated separately.

To estimate the impact of export earnings on GDP growth, I follow the procedure used by Ram (1985, 1987). Ram treated exports (X) as an input along with labor (L) and capital stock (K) in a simple model of the growth of output (GDP): GDP = f(L, K, X). He then estimated the total differential of this model,

$$GDP^* = a + bL^* + cK^* + dX^* + u$$

where * indicates rate of change and $K^* = I/Y$, the incremental capital/output ratio.

Because imported machinery and transportation equipment (MTE) accounted for an average of 62 percent of Jamaica's net fixed

Table 4.3
Coefficients of the Determinants of the Growth and Instability
of Total Exports (TEX) and Merchandise Export (MEX), 1957-1986

	LTEX		LMEX	
	Growth	Instability	Growth	Instability
Constant	-.2606	-.0002 (-1.86)	-.357 (-.0002)	-.00005 (-2.00)(-.0003)
LVSER	.309	.428 (12.14)		.444 (9.32)(7.47)
LVALU	.289	.344 (8.75)	.443 (11.44)	
LVBAX	.115	.144 (1.97)	.271 (7.35)	.268 (4.48)(3.66)
LVSUG	.260	.243 (6.22)	.362 (2.14)	.367 (6.32)(6.49)
Adjusted R^2	.99	.94	.99	.87
DW		1.26	1.97	1.79 1.89

The letter L in front of the variables indicates log. t statistics are in parentheses.

Table 4.4
Regression Coefficients of Growth Model

	Constant	LPOP	LMTE	R2	F
LGDP (1957-73)	-3.208 (-1.44)	.949 (1.72)	.548 (7.28)	.95	168
LGDP (1973-86)	-43.271 (-29.42)	10.271 (29.42)	.133 (6.07)	.99	1833
LGDP (1957-86)	-21.443 (-5.590)	5.222 (5.54)	.410 (3.622)	.94	246

t statistics are in parentheses.

Table 4.5
Regression of Residuals of Growth Model Variables around Time, 1957-1986

	Constant	LPOP	LMTE	LTEX	R2	F
LGDP	-.02573	-7.079 (-5.432)	.1049 (1.73)		.55	19.3
LGDP	-.02591	-5.318 (-5.91)		.4151 (6.570)	.81	63.3

t statistics are in parentheses.

domestic capital formation over the thirty-year period and because variations in total export earnings (TEX) explained 89 percent of the variations in MTE over that period,[2] I have replaced the variables K and X with MTE. Thus the following growth model was estimated: LOG GDP = log a + b log POP + c log MTE where POP is the population proxy for labor. The estimated coefficients for the thirty-year period and the two sub-periods are shown in Table 4.4. The coefficient for MTE is significant at the 1 percent level for all periods. Over the thirty-year period, a 1 percent increase in MTE gave rise to a .41 percent increase in GDP growth.

To estimate the impact of the instability of POP and MTE on the instability of GDP growth, the residuals from the regression of each variable on its time trend were used as data. The results (Table 4.5) show that the instability of POP and MTE explained 55 percent of the instability of GDP, with POP having a negative impact and MTE a positive one. When TEX was substituted for MTE, the instability of POP and TEX together explained an even larger share (81 percent) of GDP instability, underscoring the fact that export earnings affect GDP directly as well as indirectly through the import of capital goods.

Although over the thirty-year period, the growth of the population was far less unstable than the growth of other variables, the variable POP had a strong positive impact on GDP growth and a strong negative impact on GDP instability. MTE, on the other hand, had a positive impact on both GDP growth and instability, with its impact on growth greater than its impact on instability.

CONCLUSION

The analysis indicates that the change in the composition of exports toward a dominance of services has been accompanied by higher instability in export earnings. However, much of this greater instability of export earnings has been due to the instability of world prices and the exchange rate. Because imported capital goods are directly related to export earnings and because these goods account for the major share of net fixed domestic capital formation, changes in world prices and the exchange rate are quickly transmitted to domestic output growth. As export earnings become more dependent on the export of services, it is reasonable to expect that the growth of output will acquire more of the unstable characteristics of those services, particularly tourism.

NOTES

1. The price of aluminum in New York was used as a proxy for the world price of bauxite and alumina because in 1974 the Government of Jamaica legislated a levy on bauxite production which was based on the average realized price of aluminum in the world market. See Palmer, 1979.

2. $\text{Log MTE} = 1.145 + .818 \text{ Log TEX} \qquad R2 = .89$
     (1957-86) (6.46)   (16.03)

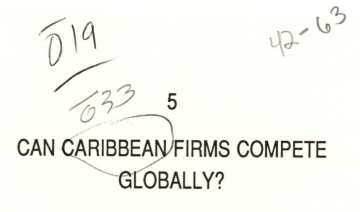

5

CAN CARIBBEAN FIRMS COMPETE GLOBALLY?

Charles M. Byles

As international competition becomes more global, certain nations emerge as having the most competitive industries--the United States in commercial aircraft, entertainment, and pharmaceuticals; Germany in high-performance automobiles and chemicals; Japan in semiconductors and VCRs; Italy in footwear and textiles, and South Korea in shipping (Porter, 1990b). Is there a place for the tiny nations of the Caribbean? Are there industries in which these countries can aspire to global leadership? Porter (1990b) has shown that international success stories occur not just in the bigger and better known industries, but also in smaller, lesser known industries such as South Korean pianos, Italian ski boots, and British biscuits. Are there potential success stories for smaller industries in the Caribbean?

This chapter seeks to examine the managerial characteristics of Caribbean firms with the intent of determining whether these characteristics help or hurt a nation's ability to emerge as competitively successful in certain industries. To do this, the focus will be on Jamaica, one of the larger, more influential nations in the Caribbean which exhibits many of the managerial characteristics of firms in the region. The chapter will also examine some attributes of Caribbean nations to determine if these attributes help or hurt in global competition.

The work is divided into three parts. Part 1 discusses some common managerial problems in Jamaican and Caribbean firms. Part 2 examines some characteristics of Jamaican and Caribbean firms as compared to a widely known model of international competitiveness. Finally, Part 3 discusses the managerial challenges for the 1990s.

MANAGERIAL PROBLEMS

Planning Process and Content

Planning in most Caribbean and Jamaican firms would best be classified as what Mintzberg (1973) calls the "adaptive mode." According to Mintzberg, four major characteristics distinguish the adaptive mode of strategy making. While these characteristics are not present in all organizations, they nonetheless reflect some typical patterns:

1. Nonexistence of clear goals. The organization is caught in a complex web of forces--unions, managers, government agencies, and employees, each trying to shape the decisionmaking process.
2. Solutions to problems are reactive (i.e., responding to problems after they have occurred) rather than proactive (predicting problems and attempting to develop solutions before those problems occur).
3. Decisions tend to be made incrementally, that is, in a series of small steps rather than in a single bold step. The decisionmaker tends to be cautious, trying only that which is familiar.
4. Decisions tend to be disjointed rather than integrated. The organization operates as a fragmented set of parts, each making independent decisions.

What are the consequences of this approach? The adaptive mode is more appropriate for larger firms that wish to "survive" or maintain the "status quo." It is less appropriate for those seeking to be exceptional in terms of developing a new product, service, or process. And while most firms at one time or another will use this mode, for larger organizations seeking to be unique, the planning mode will be more appropriate, whereas for the smaller firm the entrepreneurial mode will work best.

The planning process in Caribbean and Jamaican organizations also tends to be unsystematic in that firms tend not to go through a fairly formal set of steps. For example, definition of mission and objectives, internal and external analysis, development of a strategy, and implementation of strategy. Nicholls, Lyn-Cook, and Roslow (1990) argue that Jamaican export activities have frequently been unplanned, and not the result of well-defined goals and strategies. Especially in larger firms, where research evidence suggests that formal planning pays off, these firms tend to operate more in a centralized mode with one or a few top executives making most of the decisions based on their own personal views.

Jamaican and Caribbean firms tend to have little knowledge of the content of strategies. This is in part a result of the limited research on Caribbean firms. In the United States, for example, concepts such as the value chain and the reconfiguration of the value chain to build cost or differentiation advantages (Porter, 1985) are known and applied. A number of Jamaican firms are not guided by attempts to build lasting competitive advantages and hence end up being stuck-in-the-middle (i.e., having neither a cost nor differentiation advantage).

When considering the actual kinds of strategies followed, Caribbean firms would best be classified as "defenders" or "reactors" (Miles and Snow, 1978). The defender organization attempts to identify a narrow and stable product area in which it competes on the basis of lower prices or superior quality or services. This organization is risk-averse, that is, it sticks to what it knows, and rarely moves into unfamiliar product areas. This strategy would be a characteristic of most successful firms in the region (in Jamaica, for example, firms in the insurance and banking industries, hotels, some light manufacturing, and distribution). In comparison, the reactor organization does not have a consistent approach to competing (i.e., it does not have competitive advantages based on lower cost or uniqueness). This organization tends not to shape industry events by acting on its own initiative, but rather responds to changes generated by other firms. Some of the less successful industries in the Caribbean, many of which survive with significant subsidies, fall into this category (in Jamaica, the sugar and banana industries, and some of the quasi-governmental organizations).

Structure

Most medium- and large-sized Caribbean firms tend to be bureaucratic (i.e., formalized, hierarchical, centralized). This is generally a result of inheritance of centralized political structures from British colonialism and the general lack of individual independence as a cultural trait in the region. But not all organizations are bureaucratic. Smaller entrepreneurial firms in the distribution sector as well as small firms engaged in automobile and electrical repair tend to be more organic (i.e., less formalized, few hierarchical levels, decentralized). These firms tend to be more responsive or adaptive.

The structural concept that best captures the Caribbean firm is found in Mintzberg's (1979) *The Structuring of Organizations*. Most larger business organizations fit either of Mintzberg's two kinds of bureaucracy, machine (e.g., manufacturing firms, banks) or professional (e.g., hospitals, schools, public accounting and architectural firms). While these organizations are designed for efficiency, their main weakness is the inability to respond to change. To make matters worse, when a defender strategy is combined with a bureaucratic structure, the result is a "status quo" organization that takes few risks. Herein lies the source of former Jamaican Prime Minister Manley's criticism that some Jamaican managers were "singularly unenterprising and timid" (Manley, 1990). This comment reflects the widespread view that Caribbean organizations are copycats of American, British, or Canadian ideas rather than engaging in risk-taking to create new products or new production processes. To some degree, Manley's criticism of Jamaican firms as having a "trader mentality" (Manley, 1990) emphasizes the tendency of firms to take the safer and easier route. Perhaps the trader mentality also reflects the concern of the business person about economic instability and the need to make a quick return with as little investment as possible.

In contrast to the machine and professional bureaucracies that dominate Caribbean industries is the Simple Structure. This is unique for what it does not have--bureaucratic characteristics. The Simple Structure is found in the hundreds of small businesses ranging from the small grocery store to the corner tailor's shop. These organizations are, by necessity, flexible and adaptive. And while they do not come up with technologically sophisticated solutions to problems, their main strength is the ability to survive with limited resources. Thus the small mechanic or body shop learns to make repairs with limited replacement parts. Or the Jamaican ICI (informal commercial importer known in the local jargon as a "higgler") learns to find cheap foreign exchange and inexpensive suppliers of her products.

The dilemma is that the major economic engines in these countries are mostly designed for conditions of moderate change when drastic change is needed. The less significant economic entities are designed for change, but their energies are focused on coping with the irrationalities of the economic and political system. Or put another way, the higgler's creative energy is directed at hustling or beating a needlessly inefficient system rather than creating a substantive product or service that would advance the productive capacity of the country.

Entrepreneurial Behavior

Caribbean firms and Jamaican firms in particular tend to be risk-averse in that they tend to do in Jamaica that which has been tried elsewhere. Berger (1984) reports on the words of a Jamaican who said, "We don't really have capitalists here, we have bazaar merchants" (9). Manley (1990) attributes this behavior in part to what he calls a system of "irrelevant education" which produces great skill in the fields of medicine, law, politics, and the arts, but great weaknesses in skills related to increasing economic performance. He also blames the colonial history of Jamaica which created in people a lack of confidence in doing things for themselves. Worrell (1987), in a sharp indictment of Caribbean nations, stated, "In general, Caribbean societies do not seem receptive to innovation. For many years it was thought that the region lacked entrepreneurs. It now seems more likely that these societies fail to recognize entrepreneurs when they see them." He went on to say, "Genuine inventiveness, organizing ability and perseverance have been demonstrated in informal markets, in religious organizations, in sports clubs, and in educational institutions. However, throughout the English-speaking Caribbean, the dominant economic institutions have been hostile to the development of this entrepreneurship, which remains largely untapped" (25).

But, is imitation necessarily an inappropriate approach for Caribbean firms? Should one expect firms to be truly innovative in the sense of coming up with brand new products or processes? Or is it more realistic to expect some imitation of existing products with some value added? Imitation may be a viable approach, but only if along the lines of what some Japanese or Korean firms have done. Japanese firms like Matsushita have taken existing products such as TVs or VCRs and enhanced them by adding features or improving reliability. In contrast, Korean firms have taken similar products and sold them as low cost, less sophisticated, standardized products (e.g., Gold Star, Samsung). Thus imitation is a viable strategy, but it must be *innovative* imitation (Levitt, 1986) in which the imitated product is either of higher quality or can be sold at a lower price. And while Caribbean firms may not be prepared to do this in electronics, the principle is applicable in wide ranges of industries such as furniture, aquaculture, light manufacturing, or services.

Work Attitudes and Motivation

While local business people in the Caribbean complain about "lazy workers," observers in the United States praise the energy and success of West Indian immigrants. What explains this apparent paradox?

First, one needs to acknowledge that there is a problem of poor work attitudes in the Caribbean. Berger (1984) cites one of the obstacles to economic success in Jamaica as "lackadaisical attitudes toward work (a favorite Jamaican reply to the question of when something will be done is 'soon come,' roughly analogous to the Latin American *mañana*)" (9). But, are these attitudes inbred, or are they a response to a system which offers few motivating rewards?

While there are individuals that may be inherently lazy, many of the poor work attitudes are a function of inequities, absence of real rewards, and generally poorly designed and administered reward systems. Inequities occur where workers perceive their compensation as low compared to others who have contributed less. This occurs in particular between manual (low-paying) and white collar (high-paying) jobs. This results in the low-paid workers reducing their efforts to that point which they view as commensurate with their pay level. For many jobs, particularly manual tasks, few rewards are available to motivate workers. Upward mobility is limited and workers have little expectation that hard work will lead to rewards. For this reason, the common North American motivational theory known as expectancy theory (which assumes that if workers know what is expected of them and are rewarded for achievement, they will be motivated to work) is difficult to apply in the Caribbean. Finally, most motivational and reward systems in West Indian firms are poorly designed and administered. Basic techniques like goal-setting, the use of feedback, and linking rewards to performance are not properly applied. As shown by Punnett (1986), goal-setting can motivate workers to increase performance in the Caribbean. It is possible that other North American motivational techniques might be applicable in the Caribbean, but these are limited by the absence of substantive rewards and the inequities discussed above.

In general, there tends to be more respect for white collar jobs, more interest in theory than application, and more regard for managing than doing. Or put another way, the closer a particular job is to actual production, the lesser the prestige of that job. Hence, the tendency in the Caribbean to avoid hands-on jobs in agriculture, mechanics, and other productive vocations and instead aspire to law, history, and the social sciences. For those in these less prestigious jobs, the limited rewards and opportunities result in little drive or interest and hence the stereotypical lazy worker.

Leadership

Slavery and colonial rule have left the region with a politically apathetic lower economic class and authoritarian middle and upper classes. As Monroe (1972) notes, the Jamaican lower economic classes traditionally had little or no interest in influencing their country's political future and the independence movement was led primarily by well-educated elite in the country. The tendency of authoritarianism in the elite and apathy and submissiveness among the poorer classes explains the tendency of Caribbean governments toward statism and the autocratic attitudes of managers in the private sector. Although changing somewhat, this has been an entrenched cultural attitude which is similar to what Hofstede (1980a) calls "high power distance." Hofstede (1980b) defines power distance as "the extent to which a society accepts the fact that power in institutions and organizations is distributed unequally." While data were not collected on Caribbean countries in Hofstede's study, these countries nonetheless have many of the underlying characteristics of the power distance norm (such as less national wealth, concentration of political power, colonialism, imperialism, etc.). High power distance countries tend to have certain consequences for organizations (Hofstede, 1980a) which seem to be present in Caribbean organizations. These are:

1. Greater centralization
2. Tall organizational pyramids
3. Large proportion of supervisory personnel
4. Large wage differentials
5. Low qualification of lower strata
6. White collar jobs valued more than blue collar jobs

Jamaican and Caribbean firms could also be classified practicing the Theory X approach to leadership (McGregor, 1960). A Theory X manager believes that

1. Humans dislike work and will avoid it if possible
2. They must be coerced, controlled, directed, threatened with punishment to get them to put forward adequate effort toward the achievement of organizational objectives
3. The average person prefers to be directed, wishes to avoid responsibility, has relatively little ambition, wants security above all.

The Theory X concept and high power distance are similar, if not the same. In fact, Hofstede (1980a) has found significant correlation (r=.75) between Theory X and the power distance index.

What are some of the consequences of this approach to leadership? While the Theory X assumptions are true for some individuals, and in fact, perhaps, true for many workers in Caribbean organizations, there is evidence that, in general, this approach undermines initiative and drive in most individuals. Most individuals are driven by certain unsatisfied needs--physiological, safety, social, esteem, and self-actualization (Maslow, 1970). In most organizations, the basic needs are satisfied (physiological, safety, and social), and the esteem and self-actualization needs become the primary motivators. The Theory X approach, by removing an individual's ability to participate and control his environment, thwarts the achievement of these higher-level needs. Theory X becomes a self-fulfilling prophesy --its assumptions about human nature create the lazy, uncooperative worker that shirks responsibility.

Thus the dilemma faced by Caribbean firms is an entrenched attitude and style of leadership which is counterproductive but difficult to change. It is difficult to change because the Theory X assumptions are true for many workers, but practicing that style only perpetuates the attitude among workers. And when combined with unavailability of rewards and opportunities for workers, low prestige and perceived unfairness toward manual labor, authoritarian leadership contributes to low morale, worker-management conflict, and ultimately low productivity.

Implications for Global Competition

Table 5.1 summarizes the managerial characteristics of Caribbean and Jamaican firms and contrasts these with the characteristics required for success in global competition. To what extent do these characteristics support or impede the ability of firms to compete globally?

An adaptive and informal planning process is typical of an organization primarily concerned about the immediate, not the future. Such an organization is less likely to come up with bold new ideas which are necessary for developing successful competitive strategies. Because of this approach, these organizations have a strategic orientation that is weak domestically (stuck-in-the-middle and Reactor), or strong domestically but questionable globally (Defender). Porter (1990a) argues that the key to success in global competition is the choice of one of four generic strategies--differentiation (e.g., Japanese shipbuilders who offer high-quality vessels at premium prices), cost leadership (e.g., Korean shipbuilders who offer good but not superior vessels), differentiation focus (e.g., Scandinavian shipbuilders who offer specialized ships such as icebreakers), or cost focus (e.g., Chinese shipbuilders who offer relatively simple, standard vessels). But, as Porter argues, the key underlying concept to competitive advantage is *innovation*--the ability to develop new products or processes, or to improve or upgrade old ones. The adaptive mode is not conducive to

Table 5.1
Actual and Required Managerial Characteristics

	Actual	Required
Planning Process	Adaptive, Informal	Planning, Entrepreneurial, Formal
Type of Strategy	Stuck-in-the-Middle Defenders, Reactors	Differentiation, Cost Leadership, Focus; Prospector
Structure	Machine Bureaucracy Professional Bureaucracy Simple Structure	Adhocracy Simple Structure
Entrepreneurial Behavior	Imitation	Innovation, Innovative Imitation
Work Attitudes/Motivation	Indifferent, Uncommitted Inequities Absence of real rewards Poor design and administration	Committed Equity Performance-Reward Linkage
Leadership	Theory X, High Power Distance	Theory Y, Low Power Distance

the kind of innovation required for a global competitive advantage. Nor is the defender strategy. If firms wish to compete globally, they must move more toward a clear business strategy such as differentiation or cost leadership (or a Prospector strategy which is very similar conceptually to differentiation and focus differentiation).

The most common kinds of structures found in medium- or larger-sized Caribbean firms (Machine or Professional Bureaucracies) can be suited to global competition provided the competitive environments are fairly stable. The Machine Bureaucracy is a feasible structure for efficiency (cost leadership) and the Professional Bureaucracy is feasible for uniqueness (differentiation). But these structures are limited by not being responsive to environmental change. In contrast, the more flexible forms, such as the Adhocracy and the Simple Structure, thrive on change. In view of the turbulence in the national and international economic and competitive environments, Caribbean firms need to become more flexible in order to facilitate the innovative process. To do this, it is possible to maintain the basic bureaucratic forms, but create within these organizations smaller units which are designed along flexible lines (for example, a small new product development department within a larger Machine Bureaucracy).

Innovation or innovative imitation (imitation but with some significant added value) will take time to inculcate among Caribbean managers as it requires a significant behavioral change. That behavioral change can be brought about by training in how to think differently. But other changes are needed, such as incentives for taking risks, and rewards for creativity. Some failure must be tolerated. Most important, top management must support entrepreneurship within the organization in the form of public proclamations, mission and goal statements, and reward and promotion systems. Hiring, promotion, reward, and firing practices must be rethought in light of this new emphasis. Most firms have creative people, some of whom eventually emigrate out of frustration with the inability to use this talent fully. Others simply give up.

Perhaps the most limiting characteristics of Caribbean firms in becoming globally competitive are the work attitudes and leadership approaches found in most firms. The most striking characteristic of the globally successful countries (such as the United States, Japan, and Western Europe) is the commitment of their employees to quality and the understanding their managers have about the human side of organizations. Many Caribbean nations must change their attitudes toward manual work. And reward systems must recognize the importance of workers at lower levels in the organization. Training can play a role in bringing about attitude changes. Unfortunately, management training is at a rudimentary level in many of these nations. There is not as much respect for formal training since there is a widely held view that managers are born, not made. Caribbean nations need to break the tendency of thinking that change is not possible (which cripples most attempts at management training) and come to realize that one can learn to be a good manager or supervisor, or learn to be creative. Finally, managers should realize that participation increases the commitment to the task at hand. Authoritarianism ultimately hurts the organization and prevents the development of thinking, productive employees. Instead, employees become passive and uncommitted and hardly able to take on the challenges of global competition.

ATTRIBUTES OF CARIBBEAN NATIONS

The Porter Model

Porter (1990b), in an extensive study of global competitiveness, concluded that a nation's competitiveness depended on the capacity of its industries to innovate and upgrade. Four broad attributes that contribute to the ability of a nation's industries to innovate and upgrade are:

1. Factor Conditions. The nation's position in factors of production, such as skilled labor or infrastructure, necessary to compete in a given industry.
2. Demand Conditions. The nature of home-market demand for the industry's product or service.
3. Related and Supporting Industries. The presence or absence in the nation of supplier industries and other related industries that are internationally competitive.
4. Firm Strategy, Structure, and Rivalry. The conditions in the nation governing how companies are created, organized and managed, as well as the nature of domestic rivalry.

Factor Conditions

Factor Conditions can be further delineated as:

1. Human resources: the quality and quantity of personnel in various fields such as toolmakers, electrical engineers, agronomists, computer programmers, and so on.
2. Physical resources: the abundance, quality, accessibility, and cost of the nation's land, water, agricultural, hydroelectric, fishing, and other national resources, including climate.
3. Knowledge resources: the nation's stock of scientific, technical, and market knowledge.
4. Capital resources: the amount and cost of capital available to finance industry.
5. Infrastructure: the type, quality, and use cost of infrastructure, including transportation system, communications system, mail and parcel delivery, payment or funds transfer, health care, and others.

While it is not possible to enumerate the standing on factor conditions for all Caribbean firms, it is possible to draw a few conclusions about general tendencies in the region. According to Porter (1990b), while the above factors play a significant role in building a cost or differentiation advantage and hence, creating an edge in global competition, the most important factors are those that are upgraded or created (for example, skilled human resources or sophisticated technologies). In general, Caribbean nations tend to be stronger on the basic factors such as a large pool of labor or a local raw-material source such as oil or bauxite. Berger, for example, summarizes Jamaica's assets as "good agricultural and mineral resources, a reasonably sophisticated infrastructure, a sizeable professional and business middle class, the English language and proximity to the North American market" (1984, 9). According to Porter (1990b), "simply having a general work force that is high school or even college educated represents no competitive advantage in modern international competition" (78). This requirement, that the factor be *specialized*, is a significant weakness in Caribbean nations. In fact, many possess weaknesses in the basic factors themselves. Human resource skills tend to be uneven. While there is wide variation in the quality of educational institutions, the region does have some good primary, secondary, and tertiary educational systems inherited from British colonial rule. The University of the West Indies, formerly part of the University of London, is well respected in the region. But education is not widely accessible. The result is a small group of well-educated managers and professionals, and a large mass of relatively uneducated potential workers. Jamaica, for example, has an ample supply of low cost, trainable labor which has an education level above most developing countries. Combined with English-language ability, this is a strength. But, a shortage exists of technically skilled labor (Investment Climate Statement, 1990). Some strengths exist in natural resources, particularly climate (for tourism), oil (Trinidad) and bauxite (Jamaica). Knowledge resources are relatively weak, primarily because they are not specialized, nor are they technical. Table 5.2 shows the percentage of Jamaican university graduates in various fields for the years 1986 through 1988. Note that the total percentage of graduates in technical fields (agriculture, engineering, medicine, natural sciences, and nursing) was 37 percent. Of that 37 percent, 24 percent were in Natural Sciences which, although scientific, tends not to be specialized nor applied. The number of graduates in Arts and General Studies and Social Sciences was 50 percent of the total! This data, although only for Jamaica, represents a general tendency in the Caribbean for students to emphasize nontechnical fields.

Capital resources tend to be modest. Some local financing is available in most countries, and foreign investment is encouraged through various investment incentive laws. Infrastructure varies somewhat from country to country, but tends to be moderately well developed. The more populous countries like Jamaica, Trinidad, and Barbados have well-developed ports, airports, and road systems, and adequate communication facilities. Whereas the less populous islands have a poorly developed infrastructure (Worrell, 1987). As pointed out by McKee and Tisdell (1990), infrastructure development in the Caribbean Islands has been based on facilitating exports, and thus tends to be more well developed in areas of the various countries where export is a priority.

Table 5.2
Jamaican Graduates of the University of the West Indies

Major	1986	1987	1988	Total	% of Total (3 yrs)
Total	1109	1169	1057		
Agriculture	7	2	2	11	.5
Arts & General Studies	205	216	181	602	23
Education	58	61	63	182	8
Engineering	42	47	43	132	6
Law	37	36	34	107	5
Medicine	46	43	45	134	6
Natural Sciences	177	204	180	561	24
Social Sciences	204	233	197	634	27
Nursing	5	3	3	11	
		Total (3 years)		2374	

Source: Pocketbook of Statistics, Jamaica, 1989. Published by the Statistical Institute of Jamaica, Kingston, Jamaica.

Demand Conditions

Porter (1990b) argued that the character of home demand for a product or service (i.e., how sophisticated or demanding buyers in the nation were) played a more significant role in developing a firm's competitive advantage than the size of home demand. Sophisticated and demanding buyers pressure firms to improve their products and services through innovation. Porter gives examples of Japanese buyersliving in small houses and facing hot summers and high electrical costs who pressured companies to pioneer compact, quiet, energy-efficient air-conditioning units.

In Caribbean nations, two opposing forces are present. Because of the proximity to North America, and the ease of travel, communication, and the presence of tourists, many buyers are familiar with high quality North American products. Within the middle and upper economic classes, sophisticated tastes have developed which closely resemble those in North America. This is countered by the limited access to North American products by the lower economic classes (and hence, absence of sophisticated tastes). In addition, for many locally produced products and services, there are few choices, and buyers became accustomed to mediocrity. This is particularly true in service industries such as banking and public transportation. Utilities in Jamaica, such as telephone, water, and electricity are unreliable and expensive (Bernal, 1984). In general, where a buyer is demanding, the absence of alternatives and the generally felt mediocrity of some local products and services leads these buyers to "give up" out of frustration. This leads to a general lowering of expectations throughout the nation.

Related and Supporting Industries

According to Porter (1990b), home-based suppliers that are world class deliver cost-effective inputs in an efficient and rapid manner. Because of their proximity to their customers, home-based suppliers provide an advantage based on close working relationships. For example, in the Italian footwear industry, shoe producers regularly discuss new styles and manufacturing techniques with leather manufacturers. This interaction yields competitive advantages in the form of more efficient processes or higher quality products.

The benefits provided by world-class-related industries is similar. The ease of exchanging information and technology helps firms to develop new products and services which in turn contribute to dominance in world markets. For example, Japanese dominance in electronic music keyboards grows out of successes in the related industries of acoustic instruments and consumer electronics.

Caribbean firms tend to be weak on world-class-related and supporting industries. Historically, their economies have been geared to exporting staples (e.g., sugar, bananas, spices) to European countries, primarily Britain, who in turn sold manufactured products to those nations. Typically, the Caribbean nation would only be involved in one or more upstream activities in the value chain (e.g., producing raw sugar), whereas the metropolitan country would control the remaining activities (in the case of sugar, refining, confectionery, etc.). The metropolitan country would not only control downstream activities, but also related activities such as packaging, byproducts, transportation, and so on. The Caribbean has traditionally been characterized by this absence of linkages (or, put another way, absence of related and supporting industries). Manley (1990) notes that, in 1945, Jamaica had virtually no linked industries since these were all in the metropolitan country. Although there have been some changes since that time, the absence of linkages is still a weakness today. Some firms in Jamaica have integrated vertically, for example, Jamaica Broilers Group Ltd., by starting its own hatchery (to supply hatching eggs for its broiler operations) and acquiring full ownership in a local feed mill.

There have been some attempts to develop related and supporting industries. One of the benefits cited of the Free Zones operating in Jamaica is that they would encourage the development of local supplier industries in addition to the technological spillover from the Zone. But to date, this has not occurred, and the primary benefit to the country is the alleviation of unemployment.

Firm Strategy, Structure, and Rivalry

Porter (1990b) concluded that internationally successful firms in various nations employed different strategies and different ways of organizing activities. For example, successful Italian firms tended to be small- or medium-sized, privately owned, and operated like extended families. These kinds of firms were successful in consumer products such as lighting, furniture, and footwear. In contrast, German firms were more structured (hierarchical) with their top management having technical backgrounds. These kinds of firms tend to be successful in technical or engineering type industries such as optics or chemicals. Such a contingency approach would suggest that Caribbean firms have some freedom to select management approaches as long as they fit with the needs of the kinds of industries in which they operate.

Unfortunately, this view can be misleading as it ignores how the management approaches evolved. In the above European examples, each approach evolved because it fit with the demands of the industry and the various skills and interests in each nation. In Caribbean nations, as discussed earlier, management approaches have not evolved out of trial and error in various businesses, but have been uncritically accepted based on earlier practices in political systems and businesses. In addition, it is unlikely that highly bureaucratic firms with authoritarian managers and following Defender or Reactor strategies would be successful given the demands of today's global industries.

On the question of rivalry, Porter argues that strong domestic rivalry creates pressures on companies to innovate and upgrade. Local rivals challenge each other to become more efficient, improve quality, or develop new products and services. In the Caribbean, in all but a few industries like tourism, domestic rivalry is minimal. The challenges facing many firms come not from competitors, but from economic conditions (inflation, shortages of raw materials, shortages of foreign exchange), government policies (import duties, taxes), work attitudes and behavior (apathy, absenteeism), and the general difficulty with getting even the simplest tasks done. Rather than seeking to optimize product or service offerings, firms are satisfied to merely survive, even if it means producing a mediocre product or service. In many instances, particularly in service industries like hotels and car rental, Caribbean firms are at a disadvantage serving American or European clients as they do not fully understand the standards to which these clients are accustomed. Local rivals are not able to create pressures that would generally lead to an improvement in product or service quality or efficiency.

Implications for Global Competition

Table 5.3 summarizes the standing of Caribbean nations in general on each of the four attributes. Factor conditions tend to be basic, with limited upgrading when specialized factors and constant upgrading are required for global competitiveness. Small markets and moderately demanding buyers are present when, for global competitiveness, large markets and demanding buyers are required. The absence of linkages, and generally weak suppliers and related firms, exists when the presence of world-class suppliers and related firms is required for global competitiveness. Also, the conservative approach to strategy making and the bureaucracy and authoritarianism present in many Caribbean firms does not fit well with the need for boldness, creativity, and flexibility required of global competition. Finally, domestic competition is minimal and the firm's energies are not directedat upgrading quality or improving efficiency, but rather at dealing with inefficiencies in the economy.

CONCLUSION: CHALLENGES FOR THE 1990s

The challenges facing Caribbean firms are twofold. First, management approaches must be rethought in light of the new demands of global competition. In general, this means a movement away from bureaucracy and authoritarianism and an embracing of the value of human beings as a significant resource in organizations. Caribbean nations have to revitalize their labor forces by removing the stigma of manual work, by inculcating in their people an optimism that says one's future can be controlled.

Second, managers must learn about global competition by observing what successful firms in the United States, Germany, South Korea, Singapore, and others elsewhere have done and must adapt ideas to Caribbean conditions. Formal training plays a role, especially in the areas of strategic thinking and entrepreneurship. In particular, management must adopt a long term view of where that firm wants to be in the future, and how it can get there.

Caribbean firms are not in a strong position to compete internationally. The responsibility for the kinds of changes needed rests not only with the business community, but also with the political

Table 5.3
Attributes of Caribbean Nations

Factor Conditions	Basic, limited upgrading
Demand Conditions	Small markets, moderately demanding buyers
Related and Supporting Industries	Absence of linkages, not world class, high import content
Firm Strategy and Structure	Defender, Reactor, Bureaucratic, Rivalry not intense

leaders and society in general. In order for these groups to work together, they must understand the role played by the various forces in global competition.

6

AN APPRAISAL OF THE STRUCTURE AND FUTURE PROSPECTS OF THE HAITIAN ECONOMY

Yosra A. Amara and David L. McKee

This chapter is aimed at reappraising Haiti's economic prospects, assuming that the nation's political situation can be normalized. Toward that end, the current structure of the Haitian economy will be reviewed with an eye to identifying the foundations for economic development and material improvements in the lot of the Haitian population. The emphasis will be positive, not dwelling upon past failures, nor attempting to assess blame for them. Instead, a sectoral discussion of the economy will be presented. Throughout the discussion, attention will be given to Haiti's relationship to economic forces beyond its shores, for such influences have had considerable impacts in shaping the situation facing Haiti today and must be presumed capable of impacting the nation's economy for the foreseeable future.

The plight which the Haitian economy finds itself in today may seem surprising if certain historical circumstances are considered. By the middle of the eighteenth century, Haiti was said to be contributing more to the revenues of France than all of the remaining French colonies collectively (Barry, Wood, and Preusch, 1984, 333). Late in that same century, "Haiti was the richest colony in the world, producing and trading more with Europe than the entire Caribbean colonies combined" (Boodhoo, 1988, 53). By that time extensive commercial relations had developed between the Haitian planters and the United States (1988, 53).

Boodhoo claimed that the Haiti-United States trade employed about 500 ships and that food imports from the United States aimed at feeding the slaves accounted for 20 percent of Haiti's total imports (54). For its part, "the U.S. transported sugar, coffee, cotton and tobacco to the mainland and to Europe" (54). In 1803, Haiti became the second country in the Western Hemisphere to gain independence from colonial rule. With its history of strong economic performance it might have been assumed that the fledgling nation's economic future would be assured. Of course hindsight being what it is, the harbingers of economic difficulty were already in place when Toussaint L'Ouverture led the colony into independence early in the nineteenth century.

Neither the European colonial powers nor the United States seemed ready to accept an independent and economically strong Haiti. Indeed the United States, in spite of its own revolutionary heritage, had sympathized with the planters during Haiti's struggle for independence. It would appear as though a real economic independence was not a viable ambition for Haiti in the early nineteenth century, thus it should not have been surprising when Toussaint L'Ouverture signed trade agreements with England and the United States.   According to Boodhoo those agreements, occasioned by the threat of political and economic isolation, opened the country to economic penetration (1988, 54).

It should be mentioned at this juncture that the purpose of the current discussion is not to chronicle the history of Haitian economic dependency, much less to speculate on what might have happened had the nation developed a strong economic sovereignty from the outset. Instead the focus will be on the structure of the Haitian economy today with an eye toward its future. Foreign linkages will be seen as a given, as they are in all economies today, including that of the United States. In such circumstances the relevant question appears to be can acceptable levels of material welfare be attained and/or improved upon. Of course the answer to such a question will be different for every economy for which it is posed.

Table 6.1 presents Gross Domestic Product at factor costs in constant United States 1976 dollars.   In addition, sector shares expressed in percentages are supplied. Although GDP increased by 72 percent from 1960 to 1980, that rather strong performance did not sustain itself during the 1980s. Indeed by 1985 GDP had fallen from

Table 6.1
Percentage of Gross Domestic Product by Sector of Origin

	1960	1970	1980	1981	1982	1983	1984	1985	1986	1987	1988
GDP at factor cost (Millions of US 1976 dollars)	593.3	642.7	1021.6	992.2	930.4	931.2	934.6	924.0	929.2	941.4	975.7
Agriculture	44.2	44.1	33.7	34.2	35.0	33.6	34.7	35.3	36.0	35.4	32.5
Mining	1.4	2.1	1.3	1.1	1.5	0.1	0.1	0.1	0.1	0.1	0.0
Manufacturing	13.5	13.1	19.0	17.3	18.1	19.1	17.9	17.6	17.0	16.4	16.7
Construction	2.4	2.6	5.6	6.0	5.8	6.1	6.2	7.1	6.6	6.7	6.3
Utilities	0.2	0.3	0.7	0.8	0.9	0.9	1.0	1.0	1.0	1.0	1.1
Transportation and Communications	2.4	1.7	1.9	2.1	2.1	2.3	2.0	1.9	1.9	1.9	2.1
Commerce	18.5	16.2	18.9	18.2	18.6	19.5	18.8	19.2	18.7	18.9	17.5
Financial Services	5.8	6.2	9.3	9.7	9.6	9.6	9.7	9.6	9.6	10.0	10.1
Restaurants and Hotels	0.5	0.4	0.7	0.6	0.7	0.7	0.6	0.6	0.5	0.5	0.6
Housing	4.7	4.6	5.0	5.1	5.6	5.7	5.8	6.0	6.0	6.1	6.0
Government	4.1	4.7	2.9	3.4	3.1	3.5	3.2	3.1	3.0	3.5	4.4

Source: Derived from the World Bank, Report No. 7469-HA. *Economic Recovery in Haiti: Performance, Issues and Prospects.* December 23, 1988. Latin America and the Caribbean Region.

a high of 1,021.6 million dollars in 1980 to 924 million dollars. By 1988 the figure had rebounded to 975.7 million dollars indicating somestrengthening in the economy, but hardly signaling the onset of economic prosperity.

An examination of sector shares indicates an economy that has experienced a substantial shift away from agriculture without the emergence of identifiably strong leadership from other sectors or activities. In 1960 agriculture and mining combined accounted for nearly 46 percent of GDP, albeit the contribution of mining was singularly small. By 1980 primary activities represented 35 percent of a much larger economy and by 1988 agriculture accounted for 32.5 percent of GDP while mining had disappeared as a significant activity.

Normally one might expect a significant decline in the sector-share of agriculture to be accompanied by positive adjustments in manufacturing and/or services. The 20-year period beginning in 1960 did see a rather substantial rise in the importance of manufacturing as a component of GDP. From a share comprising 13.5 percent in 1960, secondary activities accounted for fully 19 percent of GDP in 1980; quite an impressive figure considering the growth of GDP over the period. Unfortunately, the expansion of manufacturing did not sustain itself during the 1980s. By 1983 it had inched above its 1980 share of a GDP that was more than 90 million dollars shy of its 1980 counterpart. By 1988 manufacturing stood at 16.7 percent of a GDP that was well below its 1980 high. Thus it seems clear that the much-heralded manufacturing for export sector did little to establish a positive initiative for the Haitian economy in recent years. In various small island economies service activities appear to provide a hope for expansion and material betterment (McKee and Tisdell, 1990). During the period beginning in 1960 and ending in 1980 it appeared that services were emerging as potential leading sectors of the economy. As a group, nongovernmental services accounted for 34.5 percent of GDP in 1960 and by 1980 they had exceeded 42 percent. Thus they appeared to be taking up a certain amount of slack in the economy occasioned by the relative decline in the importance of agriculture. Unfortunately, any optimism engendered by the rising importance of services must be tempered in view of the performance of those pursuits since 1980. By 1988 their collective share of GDP had slumped to 33.7 percent, indicating less relative significance than they held in 1960.

Although the population of Haiti is increasing, the nation suffers from a difficulty which many smaller economies are experiencing: domestic market potential in many cases appears to be insufficient to support production aimed at local needs. Of course market potential is not a simple function of population size, it is also influenced by the material status of the population. Thus poverty of the sort which Haiti is experiencing translates into an abridgement of employment opportunities directed toward supplying local needs, which in turn necessitates the importation of various items that those in wealthier nations take for granted.

Acquiring needed imports necessitates encouraging the economy to move in directions that may not be in the best interests of encouraging long-run material progress.   Imports must be counterbalanced by exports. Table 6.2 shows a breakdown of exports for the years 1980 through 1987. In 1980 primary commodities, including agricultural goods and bauxite represented slightly more than 61 percent of total exports. By 1987 the share of primary commodities in total exports had fallen below 49 percent. The decline seems even more formidable since exports in general had suffered a better than 12 percent decline over the period. They stood at 197.5 million in 1987.

Much has been written about manufacturing for export as a vehicle for the development of Third World economies. Indeed various nations have achieved notable economic success using that scenario--witness, for example, the record of the Asian Tigers. Haiti, with its proximity to North American markets, might be thought to be a logical candidate for such a development strategy. Unfortunately, data concerning manufacturing exports from Haiti in recent years display a mixed picture. In 1980 light manufactured goods accounted for 68 million dollars in exports and by 1987 the figure had risen to 128.5 million dollars, a sizeable increase. However, over that period exports of goods fashioned from domestic materials actually declined. In 1980 their value stood at 31.2 million dollars or nearly 46 percent of all manufacturing exports. By 1987 they had fallen to 26.6 million dollars or just 20.7 percent of manufacturing exports. Thus the type of manufacturing which can be presumed to be most significant to the domestic economy has been in decline in recent years. The export of products made from imported material has been on the increase and indeed has been responsible for the positive performance of light

Table 6.2
Composition of Merchandise Exports

	1980	1981	1982	1983	1984	1985	1986	1987
Total Exports (F.O.b)	226.2	158.2	195.3	195.1	229.5	217.2	216.2	197.5
Agricultural Exports	118.5	52.9	55.2	72.5	68.4	66.5	72.3	48.3
Coffee	90.9	33.1	35.9	52.5	45.8	48.6	57.5	34.4
Cocoa	4.5	3.4	2.2	4.7	4.5	6.9	5.0	5.4
Essential Oils	5.4	4.9	5.7	7.7	5.6	4.3	4.3	4.6
Sugar	6.4	0.0	0.0	1.7	6.4	4.3	4.1	2.6
Sisal and Sisal Twine	9.5	7.3	9.7	5.3	5.7	2.4	1.4	1.3
Meat	1.8	4.2	1.7	0.6	0.4	0.0	0.0	0.0
Bauxite	19.6	16.6	21.3	0.0	0.0	0.0	0.0	0.0
Light Manufacturers	68.0	79.6	98.9	100.5	124.7	126.9	129.7	128.5
From Domestic Materials	31.2	26.4	30.0	24.2	27.6	29.4	27.9	26.6
From Imported Materials	36.8	53.2	68.9	76.3	97.1	97.5	101.8	101.9
Other Exports	20.1	9.1	19.9	22.1	36.4	23.8	14.2	20.7

Source: World Bank Report No. 7469-HA. December 1988.

manufacturing during the 1980s. The impact of such operations on the economy remains to be seen.

Before discussing the policy implications of the economic situation facing Haiti it may be useful to give a brief overview of whatthe nation has been importing in recent years. Table 6.3 summarizes the composition of imports over the period from 1980 through 1987. During that time frame total imports experienced considerable fluctuation, but ended the period at 315 million dollars, down from 334.2 million dollars in 1980. Judging from those figures Haiti has been experiencing a trade deficit which adds an urgency to the importance of the export sector.

Of course the trade deficit could be cut by reductions in imports. A prime candidate for such cuts might be food products. In 1980, Haiti imported 62.1 million dollars worth of food products and by 1987 the figure had risen to 71.3 million dollars. The condition of the Haitian agricultural sector notwithstanding, it would appear both feasible and indeed advisable for the nation to reduce food imports. This goal would have to be accomplished over a reasonable period of time through a policy of import substitution in the sector in question. It may well be that Haiti will be unable to realize self-sufficiency in foodstuffs in the foreseeable future but certainly some attempt at reducing food imports seems essential, since that category is inching its way toward 20 percent of total imports. Reductions in the related categories of beverage and tobacco, raw materials, and fats and oils might also be helpful since those items accounted collectively for 13.4 percent of total imports in 1987.

With respect to other imports it seems clear that Haiti, like many Third World nations, relies heavily upon the external marketplace to procure various manufactured or processed items. Economists and others concerned with trade imbalances are often quick to recommend import substitution, high import duties, and outright import restrictions to bring down this portion of the import imbalance.

It would appear that caution may be indicated with regard to such prescriptions. Import substitution may not be a particularly effective vehicle in an economy with such a large complement of poor rural residents, not to mention an urban underclass of persons existing on the fringes of the market economy. Import substitution in consumer goods can hardly move any more quickly than economic growth characterized by the expansion of the modern sector of the economy, coupled with

Table 6.3
Composition of Imports

	1980	1981	1982	1983	1984	1985	1986	1987
Total Imports C.I.P. (Millions of $, current prices)	334.2	373.3	318.9	334.6	352.1	333.9	298.4	315.0
Food Products	62.1	81.9	72.8	79.1	79.8	85.9	69.3	71.3
Beverage and Tobacco	7.4	7.3	5.0	8.9	9.1	8.7	7.9	6.6
Raw Material	8.1	9.7	10.5	12.5	13.1	12.2	8.7	7.8
Fuel and Lubricants	61.4	64.7	55.6	61.3	61.4	63.9	50.8	42.0
Fats and Oils	24.4	27.5	15.5	29.8	33.7	31.3	33.9	36.4
Chemical Products	29.9	35.1	35.9	39.8	43.1	42.2	36.0	38.2
Manufactured Products	76.2	43.4	71.9	72.8	73.8	77.9	60.0	65.9
Machinery & Transport Equipment	87.3	105.4	89.0	74.0	80.6	82.5	63.0	70.3
Other Manufacturers	31.9	40.9	37.7	30.9	37.6	40.5	33.8	35.6
Other Items	1.7	2.6	2.4	2.6	3.0	3.9	3.8	4.1
B.O.P. Adjustments[1]	-56.2	-45.2	-77.4	-77.3	-83.4	-115.3	-68.8	-63.2

Source: The World Bank Report, No. 7469-HA. *Economic Recovery in Haiti: Performance, Issues and Prospects.* December 23, 1988. Latin America and the Caribbean Region Office.

1. Adustment for gross imports of light assembly industry products.

the absorption of labor into pursuits that generate sufficient rewards to create a customer base for products and services manufactured domestically.

Rather than import substitution, from the outset, what may be indicated is the discouragement of the importing of consumer itemswhich could be manufactured locally as the potential market for them expands in step with economic growth. It might be particularly useful to the balance of payments if luxury imports were curtailed to some extent to make room for the continued foreign purchase of items more closely linked to the needs of economic expansion. Those last-mentioned import categories would presumably include capital equipment, materials needed for the improvement of the infrastructure, and of course items required for human welfare, such as medical supplies. It can be seen from Table 6.3 that machinery and transport equipment, items that clearly fall within the category of needed imports, have experienced considerable fluctuation during the 1980s. In 1987 they amounted to 70.3 million dollars, down from 87.3 million dollars in 1980. Indeed that category declined as a percentage of total imports as well as in absolute terms over the period.

Although the brief examination of Haiti's relation to the world economy provided here gives some idea of the nation's economic plight, a further review of the structure of the Haitian economy is needed if a prognosis for the future, not to mention policies to facilitate that future, can be hoped for. In a recent review of adjustment policies and development strategies with respect to Haiti, it was suggested that "The Haitian economy, which is highly dependent on external factors, shows a structural incapacity to sustain even a mild growth level" (Clermont, 1989, 89). Pointing to Haiti's recent dependence upon foreign donors, he went on to state that "No attempt has been made to address the structural questions," asking "Can a country like Haiti undergo real development if only short term macroeconomic measures are taken?" (1989, 92).

Haiti, like many Caribbean economies, is faced with a strong, ongoing dependence on international trade in goods and services. Imports are pervasive, involved as they are in every stage of most productive processes. In such circumstances Haiti, like other Caribbean economies, finds changes in the international environment impacting nearly every aspect of its economic structure. Indeed, in the Caribbean, trade is regarded as the engine of development. Individual economies can measure their material progress in terms of their success in the international economy. In this century economies throughout the Caribbean have been experiencing increasing difficulties in the sphere of international trade due to the weakening position of primary commodities in world markets.

In Haiti two-thirds of a population in excess of six million must rely upon agriculture for their livelihood. As of 1988 the population was only 26.3 percent urban. With such data it would appear that Haiti has not been as successful in weaning its population from the land as have various other Caribbean economies. With a literacy rate of 37 percent and per capita income of $319, Haiti exhibits an economic condition which is rare in the Western Hemisphere. Comparative data reveal that Haiti is falling further behind even the low-income group of countries in Africa and Asia (World Bank, 1989).

For economies experiencing difficulties with their balance of payments the usual prescription involves import substitution. Unfortunately, Haiti to date falls short of the level of development where such a prescription can be applied. As mentioned earlier in this discussion, the nation still relies heavily upon food imports. Clearly, any meaningful reduction in such a dependency must await substantial improvement and/or adjustments in the agricultural sector. It goes without saying that the nation's reliance upon agricultural exports in its balance of payments battle must be curtailed.

If that is accomplished through agricultural production for domestic consumption, it might be presumed that the balance of payments problem would be attacked from both sides of the ledger. Less food would have to be imported and less reliance upon unpredictable international produce markets would be necessary. These two benefits taken together would certainly reduce the balance of payments problem but would hardly eliminate it. The need for ongoing export earnings dictates that it will be difficult if not impossible to eliminate all reliance upon the export of agricultural goods anytime soon. Indeed it will have to await major structural adjustments in the Haitian economy.

For structural adjustments to be feasible it will not just be necessary for Haiti to become relatively self-sufficient in food. It must accomplish that end by becoming more efficient in agriculture. Only through such improved efficiency will the economy be able to move human and other resources into manufacturing and services. At this juncture it is by no means clear that adequate opportunities exist in non agricultural pursuits. Existing manufacturing concerns have been being faced with closures and layoffs because of difficulties in obtaining the hard currency needed for imported inputs. The assembly sector, which has been a very important component of manufacturing, performed poorly with the result that multinational firms producing goods for re-export have been electing to relocate to other low-wage nations.

A restructuring of agriculture to supply domestic needs faces several difficulties. The mountainous terrain of Haiti in consort with erosion caused by deforestation, coupled with fragmented and marginal holdings militates against agricultural efficiency. Better lands held by plantations may be more easily directed toward production for domestic needs but the exigencies of the market place may slow the transition. With more than half of the population engaged in subsistence agriculture and a level of urbanization that seems relatively low by Caribbean standards, the potential for profit from domestic agriculture may seem tenuous to would-be investors.

Profitable domestic markets for agricultural commodities rely upon the needs of elements of the population based in urban areas or at least supporting themselves in nonagricultural pursuits. Barring government subsidies to agriculture or to the potential purchasers of agricultural commodities, the profit potential in domestic agricultural markets is constrained by the purchasing power of the potential customers for those markets.

In the mainstream western literature on economic development, material progress is seen as emanating from improvements in agriculture which generate surplus rural labor. These excess workers have been characterized as migrating to urban areas where they are absorbed into the "modern" sectors of the economy, presumably manufacturing and perhaps even various service pursuits. The abundant literature on such structural adjustments had its origin in the work of W. Arthur Lewis. Neither the man nor his work require much review for those familiar with the intellectual history of the Caribbean. However, it might be well to consider the line of reasoning initiated by Lewis in assessing the prospects for the Haitian economy.

All functioning economies require a productive interplay among the three economic sectors, agriculture, manufacturing, and services. In the case of Haiti a problem exists in terms of import substitution in manufacturing. The potential market is not large enough to justify the domestic production of various goods. Thus those goods, if needed, must be imported and ways must be found to redress the trade imbalance generated by such imports. To date the burden has been shared by primary exports and manufacturing exports. Neither of these sectors show the strength to redress the trade imbalance much less to generate a meaningful strengthening of the economy. Certainly the manufacturing sector as it exists can hardly be relied upon to absorb the surplus labor which will be the inevitable result of increased agricultural efficiency and the resulting rural-to- urban migration.

Surplus labor is already evident in urban Haiti--witness the situation that is evident in the long-standing squatter settlements of Port au Prince. Additional migrants to Haitian urban areas, the majority of whom will be illiterate, can hardly be assumed to be absorbed into an export-oriented manufacturing sector and will undoubtedly swell the ranks of urban squatters. The negative aesthetics of these circumstances may obscure certain positive overspills from them.

"The fact that pools of surplus labor are growing in Third World metropolitan complexes may not be quite the disaster that it is perceived to be by those who judge the situation by the standards of advanced nations" (McKee, 1988, 39). If the urban informal sector offers survival for surplus rural population it makes improvements in the efficiency of agriculture possible. To the extent that various participants in the urban informal sector are able to earn wages beyond subsistence, the money economy expands and with it profit opportunities and the potential for the establishment of small-scale production and service facilities catering to the needs of those in the informal sector first of all, and perhaps to a small, but growing, clientele beyond the informal sector. It should be noted that such developments where they occur have little linkage, if any, to the international economy and/or the production facilities of multinational firms.

Experience in the production and service pursuits of the informal sector may lead eventually to an entrée into what is sometimes characterized as the modern sector. This progression can occur through individuals ultimately finding employment in the urban service sector or the type of manufacturing operations indigenous to Haiti, which are geared toward foreign markets. Entry into the modern sector can also result from the growth of enterprises begun in the informal sector, in which case the innovators in question (entrepreneurs?) bring their employees and/or associates with them through the transition. Even in cases where individual livelihoods remain rooted in the informal sector, it is possible for appreciable progress beyond subsistence to be achieved. Thus in the squatter settlements economic improvements may be occurring which may not always be apparent to the casual observer.

This is hardly to suggest that improved agricultural efficiency, followed by rural to urban migration and some sort of economic apprenticeship in the informal sector, will bring Haiti into the ranks of developed nations and that all that will be required will be time. Of course any successful expansion of the market for locally produced goods and services will enlarge the economy, creating more jobs and more income, which at least in theory should continue and expand the growth process. Unfortunately Haiti, like most small Third World nations, has limits with respect to what it can supply for itself locally. It will never reach a point where it no longer must rely upon substantial imports, particularly of finished products.

Since advanced nations rely heavily upon the international economy, continuing linkage to that economy on Haiti's part is not necessarily bad. It is only bad if Haiti continues to be unable to pay with exports for what it purchases abroad. It should be noted that many Caribbean jurisdictions, the majority of which are smaller than Haiti, have been experiencing similar difficulties. Whether Haiti may be better equipped in the long run to be successful in those areas where other small nations have failed remains to be seen.

One area which deserves serious attention from those concerned with the economic future of Haiti is the service sector. In various Caribbean jurisdictions, technological advancements have facilitated the emergence of that sector to prominence as an engine of growth (McKee and Tisdell, 1990). The Caribbean nations, Haiti included, may well have a comparative advantage in certain labor-intensive services. For example, the Caribbean has become a center for U.S. offshore office operations. Since services are interlinked with the rest of the economy and play an active role in the production of goods, they assume special importance to the Caribbean countries.

Haiti is at a disadvantage compared to various other Caribbean jurisdictions because of literacy levels and infrastructure-related issues. Attention to those concerns in terms of government policy will generate a better climate for developing services which can earn foreign exchange. Haiti, due to an already crowded field, may never be able to become an offshore financial center, as some of its neighbors have. However, there is little doubt that data processing and other office-related services have potential. Beyond the activities mentioned here, tourism appears to be the service industry holding the greatest potential. Assuming an improved political situation, there is little doubt that Haiti has much to offer as a tourist destination. Indeed an increased emphasis in that direction would increase the potential for the international marketing of domestic art which has already earned substantial foreign recognition.

In conclusion it can be said that Haiti's economic position, although uncomfortable, is by no means hopeless. Improvements can only come from structural adjustments in the economy, coupled with a more balanced relationship between the domestic economy and the external world. Both objectives can be pursued in consort through efforts to improve agricultural efficiency, together with the encouragement of urban expansion and the added flexibility that those objectives should bring about. From that base developmental efforts should probably favor service industries rather than manufacturing, since the latter will rely much more heavily upon imported components, thus contributing less in a relative sense to the balance of payments. The adjusted emphasis that is being suggested should improve the labor-absorptive capabilities of the economy. To be successful it will require public involvement in providing a climate (i.e., infrastructure, health services, and education) conducive to the contemplated expansion.

III

SOME REFLECTIONS ON TOURISM

7

SMALL ISLAND ECONOMIES, TOURISM, AND POLITICAL CRISES

Mary Fish and William D. Gunther

This chapter explores the vulnerability of small island economies to political crises, a linkage which occurs through the mechanism of international tourism. Political crises can be real or imagined, and tourists can react to actual or perceived threats of terrorism, coups or threats of coups, and civil unrest. While the economies of all nations would tend to be impacted by such events, small island economies are largely dependent upon tourism as their major export activity, and thus tend to be especially sensitive to world political unrest.

This chapter represents an initial effort into tracing the potential impacts which recent acts of international terrorism and war have had on small island economies. Following a discussion of the characteristics of small island economies, it categorizes political unrest and terrorist activity by their geographic impacts (local, regional or national). The next section reviews the recent literature on the impact of political crises on tourism in general. Finally, the development dilemma of small island economies is briefly discussed.

SMALL ISLAND ECONOMIES

Small island economies merit individual attention due to their unique features. According to Legarda (1984), some of the characteristics of small island economies include their small population, limited land area, small gross national product, geographic isolation, a limited manufacturing base for exports, diseconomies of scale, and a limited number of potential export markets and import suppliers.

Legarda notes that isolation can exist both because of a distant geographic location and as a result of a lack of modern transportation facilities. Small island economies may be physically close to more developed countries but economically distant in terms of their ability to efficiently service international trade. The lack of modern airports, harbors with loading and offloading facilities, and modern telecommunications can economically isolate an economy regardless of its geographical location.

A common characteristic in most island economies is that tourism is of considerable economic importance and is often the primary export earner. By contrast, in most small nonisland economies tourism plays an important role in only a limited number of instances. Even in those limited cases however, tourism tends to be part of a well-diversified economic base (Wilkinson, 1989).[1] The relatively large economic dependence of small island economies upon tourism is recognized as an important distinguishing characteristic.

According to Wilkinson (1989, 155), there are fifty-three small island economies or "micro-states" in the world. This list includes the Caribbean and Central American countries of Antigua and Barbuda, Bahamas, Barbados, Dominican, Grenada, St. Kitts and Nevis, St. Lucia, St. Vincent and the Grenadines. In the Oceania region it includes such countries as Fiji, Samoa, the Solomon Islands, and Vanuatu. In Europe the list includes Malta. These small island economies stand out as examples of island states that are primarily dependent upon tourism.

Most small island economies, particularly those located in tropical zones, appear to have few economic alternatives for development other than tourism. Wilkinson notes that "If micro-states want to increase their export earnings in order to maintain and improve their standard of living, there may indeed be no economic alternative to tourism for some of them lack other resources" (1989, 161). The conventional wisdom for small island economies (particularly those in the Caribbean) is that their comparative advantage lies in tourism and light, labor-intensive industry.

Since island economies are small in size, often physically and culturally isolated, and have the political flavor of peripheral areas, they tend to lack the power and wealth base to initiate change

(Harrigan, 1974). A rapidly growing population with limited employment opportunities often creates a relatively large unemployed, underemployed, and unskilled labor force. Generally, the natural resource base, including fresh water, may be limited to nonexistent. Legarda (1984) suggests that these problems, which are typically associated with all small economies, tend to be exaggerated in small island economies.

Micro-states, which develop a relatively large international tourism base, are nonetheless relatively small participants in a large international business. The industry tends to be structurally oligopolistic with dominant firms establishing prices and thus tourist flows. Small island economies, as nondominant firms in the market, behave as price-takers and have little influence on trade flows. Economic decisions impacting small island economies are frequently made by multinational firms with global interests.

INTERNATIONAL TOURISM CRISES

Terrorism, internal upheaval, and other types of strife all affect tourism in a similar manner. The international tourism industry is especially sensitive to political strife because travelers are often highly visible targets for violent actions (Richter and Waugh, 1986). In many instances, the economic consequences of a terrorist act targeting tourists is immediate and significant.

A number of factors explain why tourists are often the target of terrorist activity. As Richter and Waugh note, tourists generally stay in hotels which are concentrated in specific areas, are usually easily distinguishable from the local population, and therefore are easy to "target." Tourists are also unfamiliar with their surroundings and are not likely to recognize "unusual" situations. Airports represent another viable potential site for terrorist activities since they are typically populated by diverse individuals and provide anonymity and multiple avenues of immediate escape. Richter and Waugh note that international tourism represents one of the prime targets of terrorism. However, terrorist activity can have small or large impacts on tourist flows. Examples of each type of impact are discussed briefly below.[2]

Localized and Regional Events

Politically based social unrest can have local, regional, or national impacts. The terrorist bombing in Victoria Station in London which occurred early in 1991, for example, was a terrorist act designed to impact British economic life. However, that act apparently had little impact on travel beyond the choice of train stations in London. The civil upheavals in West Africa however have had the effect of largely eliminating tourism as a functional part of these economies (Teye, 1988).[3]

An additional example of how a regional political instability can significantly impact international tourism is noted in Nepal (Suraiya, 1990). During the summer months, Indian tourists, who typically represent 25 percent of Nepal's tourist totals at that time, flock to the capital city of Katmandu. It is an apparent ideal vacation spot where Indian tourists can buy otherwise unavailable international goods at inexpensive prices.[4] As a result of this trade, the Nepalese tourist industry is the largest foreign exchange earner in the country. However, in the summer of 1989, Indian and Nepalese political relations deteriorated rapidly. As a result of these political events, some tourist hotels reported significantly lower bookings with some reporting to be operating at a 10 percent occupancy rate in the summer (Suraiya, 1990). Civil unrest has a significant impact on the volume of tourists traveling to Nepal.

Other political/terrorist activities illustrate the impact of such events on tourism. In the Fall of 1985, TWA's Flight 847 was hijacked in Athens; the cruise ship Achille Lauro, which was operating in the Mediterranean, was seized by terrorists in December; and terrorists opened fire on tourists in the Rome and Vienna airports killing 22 people. In the Spring of 1986, terrorists bombed a West German discotheque and the U.S. military initiated an action against Libya. Collectively, these events create an environment that is not attractive for potential tourists.

While the empirical evidence of the impact of such events on travel and tourism is limited, there is some information which suggests that the economic impacts are significant. Hurley (1988), for example, reported a 60 percent drop in U.S. travelers to Italy as a consequence of the collective events cited earlier.[5] A poll conducted in early 1986 for *Travel Weekly* recorded that nearly half of the travel agencies included in the survey had experienced significant trip cancellations (Conant et al., 1988). Travel agents also reported that only 58 percent of those canceling their bookings chose to rebook their travel.

In another survey, Brady and Widdows (1988) measured the extent to which Europe's 1986 travel industry was impacted by the events of late 1985 and early 1986. Comparing the number of visitors during June of 1985 with the same number for June 1986 revealed a decline of 33.4 percent for England, 26.6 percent for West Germany, and 65.7 percent for Greece. Intensive advertising and price discounting on European trips were not successful in countering this impact according to Conant. The negative travel news provided by magazines, newspapers, radio, and television had a more significant impact than could be offset by intensive advertising and price discounts. Another study suggested that U.S. resorts benefitted from canceled European trips while U.S. residents who had planned trips to Europe chose Mexico and the Caribbean area as alternates (Hurley, 1988).

In spite of the dramatic loss of tourism in Europe on a June-over-June basis, tourism to both England and Greece had been restored to previous levels by August of 1986. As Wilkinson (1987) noted, tourists apparently have short memories and soon return to popular destinations once a problem has been resolved.[6]

International Events

The most recent tourism crisis has been international in scope. Operations Desert Shield and Desert Storm have had international ramifications on travel and tourism. As a consequence of the invasion of Kuwait in August of 1990, the threat of terrorism, both within and outside the Middle East, increased significantly. This, coupled with a recession in the U.S., Britain, Canada, and a more general economic slowdown in Japan and Germany, resulted in a significant drop in international travel. Gorman (1991) indicates that, in February of 1991, international airline passenger miles dropped 26.8 percent while domestic airline passenger miles fell by 5.5 percent. Gorman also reports that according to the survey, 76 percent of the respondents replied that they expected to travel domestically or abroad in the next six months compared to 38 percent who had comparable plans during the war.

In view of these dramatic drops in tourist plans, airlines, cruise lines, hotels, and car rental companies are all initiating a number of special travel promotions. In a phrase, the industry is attempting to "jump start" tourist demand in the hopes of creating some travel momentum before the summer peak season has come and gone (Gorman, 1991).

The problems associated with an "international-event" induced crisis are formidable for the travel industry as a whole. For example, in the case of Operation Desert Storm, people chose to stay at home. Unlike more limited crises in which case some redirection of travel may be assumed, "international-induced" political crises result in alternative locations for travel not being considered.

IMPACT OF POLITICAL CRISES ON TOURISM

Political upheaval of any type at a tourist's prospective destination represents a reduction in the anticipated rate of return on investing in travel to that location. Although not monetary in nature, these "disutilities" are certainly present and are incorporated into the travel decision by tourists as well as travel agents. Additionally, threats of terrorism against airline travel and destinations represent additional costs for security for the relevant organizations. These costs are often reflected in the prices for travel, hotels, and so on.

Using this model of decision making, isolated local disturbances can reduce the demand for services to and at that particular location. Political crises with larger regional impacts can affect an entire region's economy by raising costs and lowering the tourism demand throughout the region. Even when political crises are largely localized, they may still spill over and create regional impacts. For instance, Rosensweig (1988) believes that political unrest on one Caribbean island causes the whole Caribbean to experience a reduction in tourists. He argues that most Caribbean countries tend to be complements in the minds of U.S. tourists and notes tourism demand throughout the Caribbean Islands declined in 1981, following the electoral violence in Jamaica. War and international terrorism also impact the entire international tourism industry by decreasing demand worldwide. The resulting uncertainties can even spill over into domestic tourism and travel decisions.

In general, the more severe the political crises in the view of potential tourists, the greater the impact on tourism demand. Tourists' demand is very inelastic to price changes in an area torn by political strife.

When one local area or an entire region is affected by some form of political upheaval, tourists may substitute alternate destinations. Problems in European vacation spots can benefit the small island economies, while minor disruptions at one small island will benefit other small island economies (as long as they are not considered complements). International political crises, by comparison, do not leave many options for travel substitutions.

Rosensweig studied the elasticities of substitution of the Caribbean Islands, which he considered to be competing against Mexico and "sunny" southern Europe (Spain and Greece). In his study, which covered the period from 1964 to 1983, he found a high elasticity of substitution (1.78) between the Caribbean Islands and the combination of Mexico and southern Europe. This supports the supposition that a high degree of substitution exists between small island economies and other vacation spots.

Rosensweig also noted that increases in air fares and Caribbean violence both seemed to decrease Caribbean demand in favor of Mexico. He found political unrest variables in his model to be statistically significant and noted that as a possible "precursor of the effects of terrorism on tourism" in the years since 1985 (95).

Development Choices

There are a number of factors associated with tourism-based economies. First, in most instances tourism tends to be seasonal in nature. Second, it is very sensitive to external forces such as those already discussed. Third, the demand for tourism services tend to be very price- and income-elastic. This can result in the transfer of recessions in developed countries to near-depressions in small island economies. Finally, there is an argument that the linkages in the tourism industry are such that large proportions of funds flow to the multinational firms and airlines which tend to control the industry.

On the issue of the seasonal and cyclical nature of tourism activity, Wilkinson (1987) questions this instability argument when compared with other Third World foreign exchange sources.[7] He references a large body of literature and a series of models that provide strong evidence that tourism is comparably stable. Wilkinson says an essential argument rising out of examination of these models is that tourism cannot be viewed in isolation but must be considered in the broader context of national or regional development possibilities.

Regarding the linkages within the tourism industry, much of the literature on the Caribbean Island economies indicates that approximately 40 percent of the monies spent in the islands immediately leak out of country to multinational hotel chains and airlines. The industry tends to take considerable time to develop and use local suppliers with the result that estimates of the income multiplier fall in the range of 0.58 to 1.195 (Wilkinson, 1989). While such leakages would appear to be rather large, they do tend to minimize the impact of fluctuations in tourism expenditures on the local economics. Indeed, the tradeoff may be between increased sensitivity to world events and greater local impacts of tourism expenditures. However, the sensitivity of these economies to political events suggests that such an increased dependence on tourism may not be desirable in the long run. However, as Lundberg (1980) points out, the options for small island economies may be extremely limited.

Agricultural developments are often suggested as an alternative to tourism or as a means of diversifying the small island economy. In those islands where agriculture has been developed, products such as sugar and bananas face increased competition from nonsugar substitutes and low-income elasticities resulting in a very slow-growing agricultural sector. Moreover, the unstable climates in many small island economies create significant risks to substantial agricultural developments. Wilkinson (1989) notes that the most recent data indicate that agricultural production has declined in traditional areas. This may well be due to a drop in world agricultural prices associated with increased production. These problems are intensified for small island economies by their weak market positions in relationship to the world's markets.

The two critical and related issues for small island economies are (1) the sensitivity of the economy to political crises and (2) the relatively high leakages (and consequent low local impacts) associated with tourism expenditures. Increasing local impacts raises the sensitivity of the local economy to external events. To reduce the sensitivity of the small island economy and thus allow the capturing of more local impacts will require a concentrated effort to diversify the local economy. Given the nature of small island economies, this will be no easy task.

SUMMARY

The international tourism industry is highly sensitive to political crises. Small island economies tend to be highly dependent upon international tourism. It is then rather obvious that small island economies are very vulnerable to international political crises. As minor players in a large world marketplace, these small economies are often in no position to initiate significant advertising programs to offset political crises. The issue of whether or not small economies should sidestep development of international tourism because of this instability and lack of local control is moot. As noted above, some if not most of these economies appear to have few development alternatives.

NOTES

The authors express their appreciation to Doug Waggle, Ph.D. student in Finance, for his research assistance.

1. Wilkinson (1989) compares small islands' economies with small islands that are parts of metropolitan countries that lie close off shore but are part of the same government. They appear to be comparable to small Third World island countries. They share similar features such as small size and population, static socioeconomic structure, limited resource base (including energy), lack of revenue for imports, high transportation costs, lack of local markets, and lack of infrastructure.

2. Other types of events or information will also disrupt tourism, sometimes temporarily, other times for an extended season. The eruption of Mt. St. Helens had limited international tourism ramifications. It, in fact, appears to have attracted more tourists to view the eruption. The disaster at

Chernobyl was a limited impact event. AIDS epidemics in Thailand and Kenya have lessened the tourists visiting these areas for their sexual allures.

3. Richter and Waugh point out that even when tourist areas are secured to the extent possible, when political conditions appear unstable, tourists by pass the area. They use the example Jamaica in the 1970s and 1980 examples of Haiti, Northern Ireland, and Sri Lanka.

4. Suraiya (1990) describes the ingenuity of tour agents in New Delhi during the Nepalese uprising. Movements for democracy in Nepal would dump pamphlets with the week's uprising committee's agenda, and then the tour operators would schedule tours away from the areas expecting demonstrations.

5. Hurley (1988) suggests that European and Japanese travelers are not as fearful of potential political problems and natural disasters as Americans.

6. Richter and Waugh (1986) estimate that in the Spring of 1986 after the terrorist attacks in Europe and the U.S. raid in Libya, 1.8 million Americans changed their foreign travel plans.

7. Wilkinson (1987) also points out that the view that most tourism policies and development plans in these economies must be contrary to the welfare of the general populace is wrong. In spite of the limited choices, the hosts can make choices that best service their goals.

8

CRUISE SHIPS IN THE THIRD WORLD: DEVELOPMENTAL VERSUS CORPORATE FINANCIAL OBJECTIVES

David L. McKee and Abbas Mamoozadeh

In a recent discussion of tourism in the context of Third World development, it was suggested that the justification for incorporating the industry into developmental strategies was "destination and/or location specific and should be assessed in keeping with perceptions regarding potential financial and economic impacts" (Mamoozadeh and McKee, 1990). It was felt that tourism should generally be considered as part of an overall developmental package in order to avoid the pitfalls of reliance upon an industry, the fortunes of which may be beyond the control of Third World host nations.

With this general note of caution in mind the present discussion will focus upon a specific segment of the international tourism industry--cruise vacations. The discussion will be in three parts, beginning with a general overview of the size and nature of the cruising industry. Equipped with this information the focus switches to corporate objectives in visiting Third World locations. The final section attempts to assess the potential benefits that Third World nations may realize by hosting cruise ships, with an eye to understanding what place the cruising industry should occupy in their development plans.

THE SIZE AND NATURE OF THE INDUSTRY

Cruising is the fastest growing segment of world tourism. It was estimated by the Cruise Line International Association (CLIA) that

500,000 North Americans took cruises in 1970; this figure had
increased to 2.7 million by 1986 (CLIA, 1987, 5), about a 500 percent
increase in the number of passengers during this time interval. It was
expected that this figure would increase to three million by 1987 with
the worldwide demand being 4 million passengers. It has been
estimated that the potential market is between $35-50 billion (CLIA,
1987, 8).

Reasons for the expansion of cruising are more or less the same
as the reasons cited for the expansion of tourism in general. However,
there are contributory factors which set cruising apart from general
tourism activities. Year-round cruising was not feasible until air-
conditioning was installed on board and passengers could be assured
of comfortable quarters. It is only since 1970 that cruising, once
perceived to be the domain of the very rich,[1] has become very popular.
Cost reduction, aggressive promotions, special "theme" cruises,[2] shorter
duration, incentive cruising,[3] and the fly/cruise concept have all
contributed to the expansion of the industry.

The U.S. cruise market and its industry is the largest in the world,
constituting about 65 percent of the total world market. Due to close
proximity to the Caribbean, the cruise industry is mainly based in the
southern ports, notably Miami and Everglades. The port of Miami is
by far the largest, and in 1986 better than 1.2 million cruise passengers
used its facilities, whereas the comparable figure for the port of
Everglades was 237 thousand passengers (CLIA, 1987, 35).[4] The West
Coast ports serve mainly the Mexican Riviera and Alaskan markets.
The popularity of the fly-cruise concept has significantly improved the
status of major ports of embarkation such as Miami (Kendall, 1983,
365). It may be that the fly-cruise option has potential for certain
Third World ports but that remains to be seen.

Cruise ships come in different sizes and shapes. Some can
accommodate less than 100 passengers while others have passenger
complements in excess of 2,000. The recent trend has been toward
larger cruise ships with a carrying capacity of 1500 to 2000 passengers
and crews in the 700 range. This is being pursued in one of two ways:
by building larger ships or by enlarging existing ships, with cost as one
of the major determining factors. A new ship may cost more than
$100 million. Another important factor to consider is the lead time
necessary when building a new ship. Generally, there is a three-year

time lag between the signing of a contract and the first voyage (Kendall, 1983, 363).

Enlarging an existing ship and refurbishing it is a much less costly and time-consuming proposition. This approach involves adding a midsection at costs between 33 to 50 percent of the price of a new ship (Kendall, 362). However new ships tend to be more fuel efficient than the older ones.

Cruise lines offer various tour choices. There are one-day cruises to nowhere, where the ship will sail for a few miles and then return to the port of embarkation. Three- to four-day cruises are also offered.[5] These may or may not include visits to any ports of call. One-week or two-week cruises with visits to several ports of call are also available, as are extended cruises. However, the industry standard has been the one-week cruise with an expansion in the three- to four-day category. The reason for the growth of one-week cruising is that most of the passengers are Americans who have the tendency to break up their vacations into segments of that length (Centaur Associates, 1980, 22, 59).

Most of the cruises involve visits to ports of call, of which there are several different types. Ports of call can be categorized according to the functions they perform. Terminal ports are the main embarkation and debarkation points. These ports have repair facilities and provide the ships with fuel and food among other services. Terminal ports provide business for hotels, airports, restaurants, and taxis. Semiterminal ports are locations where cruise ships call to load and/or unload passengers before they reach the terminal port. Ports of call have no terminal facilities and are simply visited by passengers (Miller, 1985, 202).

Cruises are sold on an all inclusive package basis. The fee includes all expenses excluding liquor, and certain other out-of-pocket items. It is estimated that about 95 percent of all tickets are sold by travel agents whose commission ranges from 10 to 15 percent of gross proceeds. Recently some cruise lines have tried to sell the tickets directly in order to improve their profitability. The cruise industry is in direct competition with other tourist activities for the consumers' dollars. In addition to ticket sales, the industry generates some revenue due to expenditures on board. According to the CLIA, the average passenger expenditure on board was $22.50 per day (CLIA, 1987, 4).

This additional revenue at times may make the difference between a break-even operation and profits (Kendall, 1983, 390).

Most cruises include ports of call. However, since cruise line operators are in direct competition with the ports, they like to see the passengers spend their time and money on board (Kendall, 1983, 375). Since 1975 some cruise lines have been emphasizing the on-board experience instead of stressing the glamorous nature of the ports of call. They emphasize the luxury, leisure, and entertainment facilities of the ship. Prominent among these has been Carnival Cruise Lines.

The cruising business has generally been seasonal with peak demand during the cold winter months and some summertime activities. However, due to the recent increase in the number of ships and the introduction of new ships in the near future, further increasing carrying capacity, it seems that cruise operators have to function year-round to be profitable. One way to achieve this is to move the ships into different seasonal markets. Also by aggressively promoting the cruises, the tour operators can generate summer business in areas like the Caribbean. Furthermore, it should be added that the new ships are designed to serve different markets. The industry is optimistic about its future and has made investments in new tonnage to ensure that the anticipated demand is met.

It has been estimated that by the year 2000 a quarter of the entire Western European population will be aged 65 years or over. It is also estimated that in the United States, people over age 55 will constitute one-third of the population. These age groups have been the traditional clientele of cruises. They are the present two-income-earner yuppies reaching retirement age (Page, 1987, 166). Thus it would appear that the industry will continue to have growth potential.

INDUSTRY OBJECTIVES AND THIRD WORLD HOST PORTS

The growth of the cruise subsector of the international travel industry is impacting some portions of the world with ocean access far more than others. As mentioned earlier in the current discussion, the Caribbean is by far the most popular destination for cruise customers from the United States. Indeed the Caribbean basin region appears to contain the largest and most active segment of the worldwide cruising industry (Holloway, 1986, 112). On the other side of the Atlantic "the

Mediterranean remains far the most important destination for the European markets" (Holloway, 1986, 113). In addition to the Caribbean and the Mediterranean markets, Holloway suggested that "Another significant cruising market is in Australia, with a strong program of cruising to the Pacific islands" (1986, 113).

An examination of the three regional submarkets referred to by Holloway reveals an economic anomaly which appears to be inherent in the cruising industry. Many locations visited by cruise ships in the Caribbean and the South Pacific are in the Third World. Even some Mediterranean cruise ports are in poorer countries or regions. Thus the cruising industry is bringing increasing numbers of relatively affluent, if not wealthy, vacationers into contact with materially poorer societies.

There is little doubt that these contacts would be of interest to a rather diverse group of social scientists. Without suggesting that the social and cultural implications of such contacts are unimportant, the current discussion will focus more on economic and business concerns. There is little doubt that the cruise industry is having a substantial economic impact on embarkation ports located in Florida (McKee, 1988). Impacts similar in nature if not in extent are possible in other embarkation ports, dependent of course upon the nature and extent of the traffic which they service.

It would be an oversimplification to suggest the real or potential impact of cruise ship activity in Third World ports based upon evidence from embarkation ports. Nonetheless, "the concept of the cruise ship as an entrée into the tourist business can be seductive" (McKee, 1988) for those concerned with development in Third World economies where cruise ship visits are feasible. On the surface it would appear that cruise visits spell additional employment and profit opportunities for actual or proposed host nations. When those host nations are small and possess few economic alternatives it is hardly surprising if their planners embrace the cruising industry.

There is nothing inherently ominous in the acceptance of cruise traffic in Third World ports. However, it is incumbent upon those making such decisions to appraise the real or potential impact of the industry upon host economies, and more especially upon the development objectives of those economies. It must be remembered that cruise ships are operated as a business for profit. Earlier in the current discussion it was emphasized that those in the business are in a very real sense competing with their own ports of call for passenger dollars. To the extent that they are successful, the positive impacts of cruise ships upon host ports and their economies will be reduced.

Economists have known for some time of the potential for difficulties between foreign firms and host countries. In the case of foreign manufacturing firms, one of the more serious problems results from "the global basis of decision making which results in the tendency inherent in direct investment from abroad to shift decision-making power in parts of the private sector outside the country" (Parry, 1973). Another problem with such firms has been the slanting of domestic infrastructures to suit their needs, to the detriment of more general developmental goals (McKee, 1977). "It goes without saying that any involvement that such corporations may have with small island economies will reflect their own needs or perceived advantages rather than those of their hosts" (McKee and Tisdell, 1990).

In the case of cruise ship visits, the potential for problems may be less than in the case of manufacturing facilities. Yet the absence of serious problems may not be a sufficient justification for Third World economies, particularly those of the small island variety, to agree to the hosting of cruise ships. For such jurisdictions the bottom line must be some obvious developmental gain from the activity. The potential for such a gain is probably maximized by prior planning, but even in jurisdictions where the port visits are already occurring it is possible that adjustments can be negotiated that will better serve developmental objectives.

With reference to various Caribbean jurisdictions, Ransford W. Palmer has suggested that "the reduction of the import content of tourist expenditures and the expansion of tourist-generated employment are two important objectives of the expansion of the industry" (1979, 133). In jurisdictions where necessary docking facilities exist or can be built with local labor and materials, cruise- based tourism hardly generates demands for imports on a scale comparable to land-based tourism. Hotels and resorts, together with their associated infrastructures, need not be built. Thus potentially large import balances need not materialize. Beyond that, cruise tourism affords the host nation flexibility not present in land-based tourism. The land use and environmental problems related to resort development are avoided (McKee, 1988) as are "the considerable continuing costs associated with idle tourist facilities" (McKee, 1988). Facilities can become idle due to seasonal considerations as well as economic factors beyond the control of host nations, not to mention poor local management, domestic unrest, and even criminal activity. Thus the elimination of the need for elaborate capital investment is a major contribution to facilitating risk avoidance. Of course the elimination of risk in and of itself may contribute little to economic development.

There appears to be little doubt that the cruising industry has the potential to bring large numbers of visitors to certain Third World destinations without negative impacts on foreign exchange and balance of payments positions on a scale engendered by comparable land-based tourist involvement. However, those concerned with developmental objectives must also focus on the second concern raised by Palmer--the generation of employment. How successful the hosting of cruise ships may be in that regard remains to be seen.

The objectives of the cruise lines themselves may abridge the generation of employment in host jurisdictions. Despite their advertising, which often enumerates exotic destination ports, the cruise lines also emphasize on-board experiences. As has been suggested earlier in the current discussion, they are actually competing with their own destinations for the custom of their passengers. In that competition they hold very real advantages. Aside from being able to plan their own itineraries, including the number and nature of ports to be visited, not to mention the timing and duration of each visit, they can also slant their offerings in the direction of particular types of vacationers. The judicious use of market research affords them the opportunity to satisfy the needs of their carefully orchestrated clientele, thus reducing the interest of that clientele in the exotic destination aspect of the cruise package.

The policy of the cruise lines with respect to keeping their passengers on board can be seen in their response to the fuel crisis of 1979 as well as the trend toward ever larger ships. With respect to the fuel crisis, the response was to reduce the number of port visits while at the same time cutting the speed of the ships (Centaur Associates, 1980, 61). The alternative fuel-saving strategy of more port visits or more time in port was evidently not attractive to the cruise lines. Thus the fuel crisis resulted in less exposure on the part of host ports to cruise visitors.

The trend toward ever larger vessels may also cut down on the number of shore visitors. To begin with, larger ships mean a wider range of on-board commercial and entertainment options. With

designer-level shopping facilities on board, emporium ports such as
Nassau in the Bahamas or Charlotte Amalie in the U.S. Virgin Islands
may lose business. Although Nassau is in the process of enlarging
docking facilities, many cruise ports, Nassau included, cannot
accommodate the largest of the cruise ships and the even larger ones
which are being built. The necessity of coming ashore in small craft
from unprotected anchorages at sea may prove unattractive to the older
component of cruise ship clienteles.

Ironically, the appearance of the larger vessels may reverse the
situation which generated the cruise industry in the first place. "Since
the late 1950's the passenger shipping industry has steadily shifted its
emphasis from line voyages to cruises" (Holloway, 1986, 112).
Holloway, in describing the inadequacies of the vessels in service at
that time, pronounced them to be "for the most part too large, too old
and too expensive to operate for cruising purposes" (1986, 112).
Completing his indictment of existing tonnage he suggested that the
size of the ships "limited them in the number of ports they could visit
and they were built for speed rather than leisurely cruising" (1986,
112).

Holloway's prognosis notwithstanding, the trend appears to have
shifted back toward larger ships. The expanding carrying capacity of
the industry in the Caribbean basin is characterized by increased
television advertising in the United States. As additional new or
refurbished ships, with larger carrying capacities come on line, the
need to generate additional passengers may make pricing policies more
competitive. What will happen to the Caribbean segment of the
industry remains to be seen. Increasing competition may induce the
cruise lines to develop new itineraries. This may result in the return
of longer sea voyages with fewer ports of call. That scenario would
appear to fit well with the expansion of on-board commercial and
entertainment options. Certainly it would further the apparent strategy
of the cruise lines to limit time spent in ports.

Another strategy which might be adopted is a wider use of the
fly-cruise concept. A "variation on this idea started by Cunard and
British Airways using Concorde is to travel one way by sea and the
other by Concorde" (Foster, 1985, 154). The efficiency of jet travel
hardly limits the fly-cruise concept to the use of the Concorde. In the
face of increasing competition in heavily travelled cruising areas, it
might be used to open up new embarkation ports, not to mention new

destinations. Certainly it may be instrumental in encouraging more cruise traffic to the South Pacific and other previously unscheduled Third World destinations. How the changes which are occurring in the cruise industry will impact Third World host ports, present and potential, remains to be seen.

DEVELOPMENTAL CONCERNS

In the case of multinational firms proposing to locate facilities in Third World host nations, it would appear that the nations in question have far more bargaining strength than those same nations hold in the case of cruise ship visits. Of course the bargaining strength is needed in the former situation, as on-shore facilities have considerable potential for impacting host economies (McKee, 1977). In the case of cruise ship visits, impacts are much less certain. The preemption of docking facilities and the crowding of shopping areas are obvious impacts. The financial impacts and the ability of host nations to adjust them in positive ways are far less obvious.

Increasing competition and continuing changes within the cruising industry may make that industry less attractive as a continuing developmental vehicle to host jurisdictions and those working to become such. Certainly well-established cruise ports will continue to enjoy traffic. However, with the trend toward ever larger vessels, catering to package tours, and supplying a wider variety of on-board shopping, entertainment, and service options, even those ports may not be able to expect ongoing increases in the positive impact of the industry.

With the larger ships and cruise itineraries embracing fewer ports of call it is likely that reductions will occur in visits to smaller, less developed destinations. Adjustments of this type are quite possible in established areas like the Caribbean and the Mediterranean. In the changing tour climate certain destinations may find themselves with little to offer. Thus what appeared to be a way to "give host economies some exposure to mass tourism without the permanent commitment that the construction of resorts and related infrastructure would necessitate" (McKee, 1988) may no longer be an option in many locations.

Ironically the ports with the strongest positive potential vis-à-vis gains from cruise visits are often in jurisdictions where land-based tourism is already strongly entrenched. Examples are common in the Caribbean region. Provided that land-based tourist facilities are having a positive impact, further gains are possible if cruise visits provide a demonstration effect, which draws cruise visitors back for land-based vacations.

Many Third World nations which are visited by cruise ships have little that they can do to increase their benefits from such visits. Although modest increases in the length of visits may make substantial percentage changes in passenger spending on shore, there is little that host destinations can do to persuade the cruise companies to lengthen their visits. Such destinations are close to being faced with taking what they can get from the companies concerned. To maximize the benefits from cruise visits host nations should be concerned with the local content of goods and services offered to the visitors. Of course the same procedure should be followed with respect to land-based tourists.

Some gains are possible through increases in the fees charged to both the ships and their passengers. Such increases may be most practical in well-established ports. Even in those locations gains to be had through taxes and fees are strictly limited, for passengers can opt to stay on the ships, or at least to reduce their spending, while the ships themselves may alter their itineraries. In areas like the Caribbean basin, changes in fee structures would be most effective if various jurisdictions act in consort. Even where such cooperation can be accomplished the potential gains are quite limited. It can be said that it appears to be doubtful that cruise tourism can be relied upon to bring about economic development. The activity is not significant enough, and does not generate sufficient additional employment or income. The cruise passengers eat and sleep aboard the cruise ships, and their stays in the destination ports are limited. Therefore, interindustrial linkages that are very essential to economic development are lacking. However, this is not to say that cruise tourism could not be beneficial at all. To the extent that this activity diversifies the economy, it will be beneficial to destination areas, and as mentioned earlier, further benefits will occur if cruise passengers return as land-based tourists, assuming that such tourists are beneficial to the locations in question.

If competition in the industry causes a shake-out of vessels in established cruising regions it may be that the fly-cruise concept will be expanded to include additional embarkation ports. If such ports emerge in Third World settings they may prove quite beneficial to the nations involved. It may even be that the shake-out referred to above may push smaller vessels into more specialized cruising from newly activated embarkation ports. Such possibilities are in the realm of speculation. Competition may also push larger vessels into longer sea voyages with fly-cruise options and tour packages involving some land-based vacationing. These last possibilities may open up additional Third World locations to cruising. Despite the seemingly positive possibilities cited in the present paragraph it seems doubtful that Third World economies should consider cruise tourism as a major factor in developmental plans.

NOTES

1. It is estimated by CLIA that about 50 percent of all cruise passengers earn less than $35,000 annually (CLIA, *News About Cruises*, #10473PK).

2. The special "theme" concept has taken many variations. Cruise lines have arranged such cruises as jazz festivals, educational activities, investment forums and symposia, athletic colloquia, and gourmet cooking. It is expected that theme cruising will become even more important to the industry (Page, 1987, 167).

3. Incentive cruising is more popular in Europe than in the United States. Also due to non-tax-exempt status of expenses associated with conventions held in foreign-flagged ships, this market is practically nonexistent for cruise ships since almost all of them are foreign-owned.

4. It should be noted that in the same year the port of Tampa served 239 thousand cruise passengers. However, practically all of those went on one-day cruises to nowhere. It should also be noted that cruises emanating from the port of New York mostly go to Bermuda, Europe and the eastern sea coast of North America.

5. Premier Cruise Line offers a unique concept by combining four-night cruises to Nassau with three days at Disney World. This concept is designed to appeal to families.

9

CRUISE-SHIP TOURISM AND SMALL ISLAND ECONOMIES: AN ECONOMIC PERSPECTIVE

Abbas Mamoozadeh and David L. McKee

Approaches to economic development vary and economists of different schools of thought have made different recommendations. While some developmental economists have recommended the employment of light manufacturing in the developmental process, others have placed greater emphasis on heavy manufacturing as the engine for economic development (Prebisch, 1958; Portes, 1984). In recent years, however, the role of services in the developmental process has come into question and has assumed a greater part in international negotiations.

The service industry of interest in this study is cruise-ship tourism. This activity does not require the type of investment in infrastructure that stay-over tourism requires (McKee, 1988). It creates less pressure on hard-earned foreign currency and thus may be quite appealing to local authorities.

While cruising is the fastest growing segment of the tourism industry, empirical studies on its potential impact are lacking. The purpose of this study is to investigate the impact of this activity on certain Caribbean Islands, namely: Antigua, Dominica, St. Christopher, St. Lucia, and St. Vincent. They are among the Leeward and Windward Islands,[1] and share certain facets with each other. They belong to the Organization of East Caribbean States, with the East Caribbean dollar as their currency, which has been set equal to US$ 2.7 since 1976. The main crop of the Leeward Islands is sugar, while that of the Windward Islands is bananas.

Model

The model used in estimating the impact of cruise tourism is of the Keynesian demand-based variety following the work of Ghali (1976), Jud and Krause (1976), and Archer (1984). It is designed to estimate both the direct and indirect impact of cruise tourism on the income level. This model is similar to the model used by Ghali in estimating the impact of tourism on the rate of growth of income in Hawaii.

The model consists of the following equations:

$$Y = C + I + G + X - M \tag{1}$$

where the arguments of this first equation, which is an identity, are defined as:

$$
\begin{aligned}
C_t &= c_0 + c_1 Y + R & (2)\\
I_t &= i_0 + i_1 Y_{-1} + i_2 TA_{-1} + i_3 CT_{-1} + S & (3)\\
G_t &= g_0 + g_1 Y_{-1} + g_2 TA_{-1} + g_3 CT_{-1} + U & (4)\\
X_t &= x_0 + x_1 Y_f + x_2 TA + x_3 CT + V & (5)\\
M_t &= m_0 + m_1 Y + m_2 TA + m_3 CT + W & (6)
\end{aligned}
$$

where Y is the level of gross domestic product; C is consumption expenditures; I is gross domestic investment; G is government expenditure; X is exports; M is imports; TA denotes the noncruise tourist arrivals; CT refers to cruise tourist arrivals; YF is the foreign income--U.S., and R, S, U, V and W are stochastic terms. The reason for using the U.S. income is that a good portion of international transactions are with the United States. Hence, the United States' GNP will be employed as a proxy for foreign income.

In order to simulate the level of GDP, equations (2) through (6) were substituted into equation (1) and then the resulting equation was manipulated to obtain the following.[2]

$$
\begin{aligned}
(1-c_1+m_1)\,Y &= (c_0+i_0+g_0+x_0-m_0) + (i_1+g_1)\,Y_{-1} + (x_2-m_2)\,TA \\
&\quad +(i_2+g_2)\,TA_{-1} + (x_3-m_3)\,CT + (i_3+g_3)\,CT_{-1} + x_1\,Y_f
\end{aligned} \tag{7}
$$

By dividing these coefficients by $(1-c_1+m_1)$ and designating the resulting coefficients by A's and adding an error term, equation (8) was generated:

$$Y = A_1 + A_2 Y_{-1} + A_3 TA + A_4 TA_{-1} + A_5 CT + A_6 CT_{-1}$$
$$+ A_7 Y_t \tag{8}$$

This equation was employed to estimate the coefficients and to simulate the level of gross domestic product under the current situation and also in making the counter-factual assumption that cruise tourism would have stayed at zero level. Upon the estimation of equation (8), first the level of GDPs were estimated using historical data. Following that, the GDPs were re-estimated, holding the level of cruise tourism at zero. The difference between these two predicted values of gross domestic product is attributed to the impact of cruise tourism and indicates both its direct and indirect effects. If cruise tourism has had a positive impact on the economy and this activity has increased over time, one would expect the level of income to be lower under the counter-factual assumption that cruise tourism does not exist.

Results

Table 9.1 contains the time intervals and the means of the variables for the countries under study. Considerable amounts of multicollinearity among the variables were exposed. The Principal Components (PC) technique was employed in dealing with this. In deciding the appropriate number of the PCs, McCallum's (1970) criterion was employed. McCallum has stated that the number of the PCs that minimizes the MSE should be used in the estimation process. The number of components used in estimating the regression equations are reported in Table 9.2. The Durbin-Watson statistics for the OLS estimation indicated serial correlation for St. Lucia and St. Vincent at 5 percent, two-sided test. Pagan's approach was used in re-estimating the regression equations for these two places and these are the equations which are used in estimating the impact of cruise-ship tourism (see Table 9.2).

The estimated coefficients for cruise-ship tourism and its lagged variable are all positive with the exception of that for St. Lucia and St. Vincent. However, at the 5 percent significance level, the t test indicated that, with the exception of coefficients for St. Vincent and the lagged value of cruise ships for St. Lucia, the cruise-ship coefficients

Table 9.1
Time Interval and Means of Variables

	Antigua	Dominica	St. K.	St. L.	St. V.
Time	1970-86	1970-86	1975-87	1975-87	1975-86
Means:					
GDP	254.17	136.7	154.2	345.2	195.3
GDP1	226.95	122.0	138.2	310.5	173.0
TA	89.94	17.8	35.6	82.0	30.0
TA1	84.69	17.0	31.2	76.9	27.7
CT	64.05	4.6	15.3	54.9	31.0
CT1	57.64	3.9	13.1	52.4	29.2
Yf	6438200.00	same	same	same	same

Table 9.2
Regression Results

	Const	GDP1	TA	TA1	CT	CT1	Yf	R2	R2	U
Antigua:										
	-81.5	.477	1.18	.117	.081	.27	.000014	.99	.99	.025
SE	18.7	.124	.364	.097	.169	.20	.000004			
t	-4.46	3.83	3.24	1.21	.476	1.38	3.819		DW= 2.83	
					No. of Components = 5					
Dominica:										
	8.74	.794	.254	-1.42	.143	1.21	.0000007	.99	.98	.20
SE	9.24	.092	.434	.453	.246	.602	.000002			
t	.947	8.64	.586	-3.14	.581	2.12	3.119		DW= 2.57	
					No. of Components = 5					
St. Christopher:										
	11.83	.144	2.37	.55	.499	.157	.000001	.98	.99	.019
SE	21.44	.22	.653	.13	.58	.427	.000005			
t	.551	.655	3.63	4.23	.86	.367	.2402		DW= 3.093	
					No. of Components = 5					

Table 9.2
Regression Results (Continued)

	Const	GDP1	TA	TA1	CT	CT1	Yf	R2	R2	U
St. Lucia:[1]										
	1.8	.82	.257	.275	-.109	.198	.000005	.99	.95	.017
SE	18.06	.111	.058	.049	.082	.083	.000006			
t	.099	7.36	4.39	5.58	-1.33	2.39	.781		DW= 1.95*	

No. of Components = 3

	Const	GDP1	TA	TA1	CT	CT1	Yf	R2	R2	U
St. Vincent:[1]										
	-35.83	.883	.206	-.021	-.142	.208	.000009	.97	.99	.038
SE	18.22	.229	.054	.005	.037	.054	.000099			
t	-1.97	3.85	3.85	-3.85	-3.86	3.85	.089		DW= 2.05[1]	

No. of Components = 2

1. The coefficients are estimated by using Pagan's approach to deal with serial correlation.

are not significant for other islands. The R^2s and adjusted R^2s were all high.

The following two tests as suggested by Theil (1961) were performed in order to determine the acceptability of the model:

A) The actual level of GDP was regressed on the estimated level of GDP.

$$Y_A = a + b(Y_p) + e_i \qquad (9)$$

where YA is the actual level of GDP and YP is the predicted GDP level determined by equation (8). A high R^2 indicates that the model has predictive capability and could be used in estimating the GDP level.

B) Theil's inequality coefficient was also employed to check the model for its reasonableness and predictive capabilities. In estimating this coefficient, once again the actual and predicted GDPs were employed.

$$U = \sqrt{(1/n \; \Sigma(Y_{pi} - Y_{Ai})^2)^{\frac{1}{2}}} \, / \, ((1/n \; \Sigma Y_{pi}^2 + 1/n \; \Sigma Y_{Ai}^2))^{\frac{1}{2}} \qquad (10)$$

The value of Theil's coefficient falls between zero and one. The closer this value is to zero, the greater the capability of the model in predicting the GDP level. On the other hand, a value close to one implies that the model is not performing well and has low predictive power, indicating that the model should not be used in estimating the GDP level.

These two variables were estimated for each location and they are reported as the last two columns of Table 9.2. It should be noted that the first test resulted in high R^2s and low values for Theil's U coefficient, indicating that the estimated equations had predictive power.

At this stage the GDPs were estimated, once by using historical data for cruise-ship activity and the second time by assuming it to be equal to zero. The difference between these two estimated GDPs is due to the direct and indirect impacts of cruise tourism. The results are shown in Tables 9.3 and 9.4. The results show that cruise tourism has had a positive impact in Antigua, Dominica, and St. Christopher, with the largest impact being in Antigua. It also indicated that the impact as a

Table 9.3
Impact in Millions of East Caribbean Currency

	Antigua	Dominica	St. K.	St. L.	St. V.
1971	8.49	1.03			
1972	15.56	1.43			
1973	21.87	2.13			
1974	16.81	2.80			
1975	9.71	2.35			
1976	9.04	0.62	2.35	3.02	1.76
1977	11.84	3.39	0.99	4.21	-0.01
1978	14.08	10.17	1.21	9.60	1.31
1979	20.03	10.03	1.85	7.47	1.42
1980	28.07	10.50	3.40	4.46	-0.29
1981	38.74	9.75	6.39	9.68	2.02
1982	36.69	6.98	7.39	0.05	2.87
1983	22.66	3.74	13.27	3.05	1.13
1984	19.76	7.89	20.82	2.51	-1.90
1985	26.61	4.85	21.43	1.35	8.52
1986	37.76	9.66	18.73	4.47	1.67
1987	----	----	20.21	2.49	-----

Table 9.4
Impact as a Percent of GDP

	Antigua	Dominica	St. K.	St. L.	St. V.
1971	8.85	2.40			
1972	14.24	3.14			
1973	18.50	4.29			
1974	12.78	4.92			
1975	6.83	3.90			
1976	6.69	0.83	3.11	1.91	2.21
1977	7.29	3.45	1.23	2.28	-0.01
1978	7.61	8.35	1.31	4.33	1.05
1979	8.55	8.22	1.72	2.74	1.04
1980	10.00	6.60	2.62	1.46	-0.18
1981	12.15	5.46	4.25	2.84	1.03
1982	10.61	3.58	4.65	0.01	1.28
1983	6.40	1.75	8.38	0.80	0.46
1984	4.45	3.32	11.19	0.61	-0.70
1985	5.51	1.89	10.64	0.29	2.89
1986	7.16	3.51	7.71	0.88	0.53
1987	----	----	7.60	0.46	-----

percentage of GDP has increased over time in St. Christopher and that perhaps cruise tourism is assuming a greater role in the economy. The impact in St. Lucia, although positive,is very small in relation to GDP. It is of interest to note that, although the coefficients for cruise tourism were significant for St. Vincent, the impact is very negligible and at times negative (see Table 9.2).

SUMMARY

The results seem to suggest that cruise tourism has benefitted Antigua and St. Christopher and that the impact has been increasing in the latter country. This is occurring in spite of the fact that the coefficients for cruise-ship tourism were not significant for Antigua, Dominica, and St. Christopher. On the other hand, cruise tourism has had a marginal effect in St. Vincent and St. Lucia.

The results seem to indicate that the impact of cruise tourism is destination-specific and the reasons for the positive impact in Antigua and St. Christopher is that these two islands are more dependent on tourism than the other islands. The results of the current investigation appear to be consistent with those of an earlier study which showed some positive impacts from cruise tourism for the small island nations in question, while not extending much hope for the industry becoming anything like a developmental bonanza (McKee, 1988). Antigua may be in somewhat stronger position with respect to cruise tourism because of its location and its available infrastructure. Although theoretically there may be gains to be had by the other islands in question through increased involvement in cruise tourism, such positive potential may be limited by small per capita outlays on the part of cruise visitors, coupled with the fact that the numbers of such visitors have themselves been limited.

On the policy level it may be prudent to reiterate a recommendation of the earlier study to the effect that "smaller destinations would be better served by encouraging the upper end of the cruising market" (McKee, 1988, 75). Certainly the destinations in question should benefit by such a policy. Indeed it may be feasible that Antigua with its yachting tradition might even gain from assuming the role of a hub from which smaller, upscale cruising craft might access the other islands under discussion, not to mention additional similar destinations.

NOTES

1. The Leeward Islands consist of Antigua and Barbuda, Anguilla, Montserrat, and St. Kitts-Nevis, while the Windward Islands encompasses Dominica, Grenada, St. Lucia and St. Vincent, and the Grenadines.

2. The model consists of the following equations:

$$Y = C + I + G + X - M \tag{1}$$
$$C = c_0 + c_1 Y + R \tag{2}$$
$$I = i_0 + i_1 Y_{-1} + i_2 TA_{-1} + i_3 CT_{-1} + S \tag{3}$$
$$G = g_0 + g_1 Y_{-1} + g_2 TA_{-1} + g_3 CT_{-1} + U \tag{4}$$
$$X = x_0 + x_1 Y_f + x_2 TA + x_3 CT + V \tag{5}$$
$$M = m_0 + m_1 Y + m_2 TA + m_3 CT + W \tag{6}$$

Now by substituting for the arguments of the first equation from the remaining equations and ignoring the error terms, we will have:

$$
\begin{aligned}
Y = {}& c_0 + c^1 Y + i_0 + i_1 Y_{-1} + i_2 TA_{-1} + i_3 CT_{-1} + g_0 + \\
& g_1 Y_{-1} + g_2 TA_{-1} + g_3 CT_{-1} + x_0 + x_1 Y_f + x_2 TA + \\
& x_3 CT - m_0 - m_1 Y - m_2 TA - m_3 CT
\end{aligned}
\tag{7}
$$

Now by adding the terms, we will have:

$$
\begin{aligned}
(1 - c_1 + m_1)Y = {}& (c_0 + i_0 + g_0 + x_0 - m_0) + (i_1 + g_1) Y_{-1} \\
& + (x_2 - m_2)TA + (i_2 + g_2)TA_{-1} + (x_3 - m_3)CT \\
& + (i_3 + g_3)CT_{-1} + (x_1)Y_f
\end{aligned}
\tag{8}
$$

$$
\begin{aligned}
Y = \{ & (c_0 + i_0 + g_0 + x_0 - m_0) + (i_1 + g_1) Y_{-1} + (x_2 - m_2)TA + (i_2 + g_2) TA_{-1} \\
& + (x_3 - m_3) CT + (i_3 + g_3) CT_{-1} + (x_1) Y_f \} / (1 - c_1 + m_1)
\end{aligned}
\tag{9}
$$

By designating the coefficients by A's, equation (9) can be written as:

$$Y = A_1 + A_2 Y_{-1} + A_3 TA + A_4 TA_{-1} + A_5 CT + A_6 CT_{-1} + A_7 Y_f \tag{10}$$

IV

FOREIGN LINKAGES AND GROWTH

10

THE UNITED STATES DOLLAR AND SMALL CARIBBEAN ECONOMIES

Yosra A. Amara

This study examines the exchange rate policies of selected Caribbean countries with an eye to judging them by their exports performance. The effects of tying the Caribbean countries' currencies to the U.S. dollar will be highlighted and analyzed. Exchange rate policies available for small developing countries, as those of the countries under investigation, will be presented. Moreover, the economic role of an efficient exchange rate regime and a sound financial policy will be discussed. The Caribbean countries that have been chosen are: the Bahamas, Barbados, Belize, the Dominican Republic, Guyana, Haiti, Jamaica, and Trinidad and Tobago.

The questions to be addressed are: do most Caribbean countries conduct all or nearly all their trade and financial transactions with one major industrialized country, and what exchange rate policy should Caribbean countries pursue?

In small Caribbean countries, where economies of scale limit the range of products which can be produced efficiently for small local markets, the international market is more important than in large countries which enjoy more options. It seems that international trade has greater impacts in smaller, more trade-dependent countries. The tendency is well known for the ratio of a country's trade to its GNP to be higher, the smaller is the economy. The extent to which a producer is dependent on exports for selling his manufactures obviously varies, but would appear to be greater the smaller is the domestic market and the more capital- or skill-intensive the product

(Thomas, 1982). Moreover, as growth proceeds, in very small countries, there is every indication that the degree of openness will become even greater. The process of growth requires that the ratio of exports to GNP increases because the domestic market is too small for domestic production to achieve economies of scale, and because efficient utilization of the domestic resource base requires a larger market than just the domestic one (Bond, 1979).

The export competitiveness of all but two CGCED (Caribbean Group for Cooperation in Economic Development) countries, namely Jamaica and the Dominican Republic, deteriorated markedly over much of the period between 1980 and 1987. There are two possible explanations of the changes in competitiveness of export. The first explanation is the external shift in the real exchange rates of major trading partners or competitors. The second can be due to changes in internal factors such as labor productivities, wages, national economic management, or the attractiveness of the investment/ business climate.

The primary objective of this paper is to analyze the effect of the single overriding external factor which is the peg of most CGCED countries' currencies to the U.S. dollar.

Friedman and Meltzer (1973) believe that the ideal situation for a small open economy is to peg to the currency of the country with which it has most of its trade and financial relations. Thus Caribbean countries are expected to peg to the U.S. dollar. If the international trade and financial flows are exclusively with the United States, fluctuations between the dollar and other key world currencies will matter little to the small Caribbean country. In the mean time the exchange rate between the United States and the rest of the world will be largely a matter of indifference to the small country. Once some trade and financial flows are allowed between the small country and other large countries (in essence that the small country is faced with more than one key currency to deal with), matters change. If a disturbance in one or another of the large countries is allowed to modify the exchange rate between the large countries, the impact on the effective exchange rate of the small country and on the real value of its foreign debt and exchange reserves will be felt at once.

From 1980 to 1985, the dollar appreciated sharply against the yen, the mark, and other European currencies. The change in the exchange rate was not matched by a change in relative price levels. Nor did the change in the exchange rate correspond closely to a change in relative money supplies. And from mid-1982 until March 1985, the dollar continued to appreciate even though money growth was as rapid in the United States as abroad. The dollar appreciated enormously in real terms (Frankel, 1985).

The impacts on Caribbean countries' exports were negative and caused profit squeezes on sugar exports to the European Community. Moreover, there was a disincentive for developing new exports for the European Community and Japanese markets. Competition in North American import markets was intensified from countries whose real exchange rates had not appreciated as rapidly as the CGCED's. Fortunately, until 1985 the relative decline in price-sensitive CGCED manufactured exports to nondollar areas (i.e., to the European Community) was accompanied by similar shifts in both world and developing country trade as well. The United States and Canada were booming markets. Between 1980 and 1985, before the dollar depreciated, the share of U.S. imports of the three major markets' imports rose by two-thirds while the European Community's share fell.

For the Caribbean countries, if the exchange rate had been kept fixed when the United States contracted, Caribbean countries would have suffered a loss in export demand resulting in lower levels of output and inflation than desired. They would have responded with policies to increase expenditure. The expansion would necessarily be concentrated relatively more in the nontradable sector. To achieve a better balance between the two sectors, Caribbean currencies would have to depreciate against the dollar to make the exportable sector more competitive. The appreciation of the dollar hurt output and employment in Caribbean export and import-competing industries. It also meant higher import prices for Caribbean trading partners.

Consequently, the pegged rate system cannot entirely insulate the economy. The reason lies in the high level of external trade in relation to domestic production in many small Caribbean countries. Exchange rate changes cannot prevent the level of economic activity in one country from being affected directly by the demand for its products by its principal trading partners. Those responsible for economic policies need to continue to take a close interest in economic development in other countries.

Providing that the economy is starting from a position of monetary and exchange-rate equilibrium, the national money supply should expand above its norm when the currency becomes unexpectedly strong in the foreign exchanges and contract when it is weak. Whether or not the underlying disturbances are real or monetary does not matter. This rule is surprisingly robust in mitigating unexpected inflations or deflations, and has the incidental advantage of making foreign trade more efficient by smoothing exchange-rate fluctuations. If followed by a "small" open economy (not using the inflation tax) whose own money supply is negligible in relationship to the relevant hard-currency outside world, such an exchange rate rule by itself is sufficient to maintain monetary equilibrium (McKinnon and Mathieson, 1981).

In choosing fixed over flexible exchange rates, a country gives up the right to have control over the value of its currency. Moreover, it cannot determine its own rate of inflation.

When allowing the Caribbean currency (for example, the Jamaican dollar) to fall in terms of other currencies, Jamaican goods can become cheaper to foreigners. Similarly, foreign goods can become more expensive to a Jamaican. Changes in exchange rates can therefore alter the relative price of Jamaican and foreign goods in precisely the same way as can changes in internal prices in Jamaica and in foreign countries.

In 1986, of total CGCED countries' exports, 85 percent went to the United States, 12 percent to the European Community, and 4 percent went to Canada (International Monetary Fund, 1989b). Similar trends have taken place on the import side (International Monetary Fund, 1989b). Trade diversification makes it difficult for one to take such a narrow view of the Caribbean countries' currency arrangements. Once actual and expected trade and financial diversification is introduced, discussions on exchange rate policy and financial management for Caribbean countries, particularly the smaller ones, become more difficult. With their trade and financial diversification would they be better off to peg their currencies to the U.S. dollar, the Canadian dollar, the French Franc, or the British pound, or some kind of a weighted average of the four? In the simplest extreme case, pegging to the currency of one major country (the U.S. dollar) tied the small Caribbean country price level to the level of the United States yet left it invariant to changes among key currency values and price levels in the rest of the world, especially the European Community, Canada, and Japan. Now, no pegging to any single currency will achieve the objective of insulating the Caribbean price level from fluctuations among key currencies. Put another way, under conditions of diversification pegging to a single key currency will result in variations in the effective exchange rate of the small country. Those variations will result from fluctuations among key currencies and will have nothing to do with the balance-of-payments position of the small country.

To reduce its loss of control over its effective exchange rate, the small Caribbean country will have to peg to a weighted average of key currencies. If the goal is to keep domestic prices in line with the "world" price level, the weights will have to correspond to those of each major country contributing to such a price level.

Table 10.1 shows the change in competitiveness of some CGCED members when their exchange rate is compared to their competitors for specific products, weighted by each competitors' share of world exports of that product. The average real exchange rate of all competitors is kept at 100 for all years. While many competitors also peg to the dollar, and few of them appreciated significantly against it, only the Dominican Republic and Jamaica remained at or below the average of their competitors. In all major products checked, by 1986, the other CGCED members had appreciated 40 percent or more than their competitors since 1980. Jamaica and the Dominican Republic were the major exception. Although suffering during the first part of the period from dollar appreciation like the rest of the CGCED countries, by the end of the period their real exchange rates had depreciated significantly below their 1980 levels. Jamaican and Dominican manufactured exports grew rapidly after their real devaluation occurred. In fact, before 1984, they had been growing slower than the CGCED average, after devaluation they grew almost five times faster (The World Bank, 1988).

In spite of devaluation, no CGCED country has actively used the real exchange rate as a significant export-promotion instrument. Real exchange rate changes occurred only after severe disequilibrium caused by economic mismanagement. The extreme openness of the small CGCED economies and their lack of individual control over their nominal exchange rates makes real exchange rate shifts difficult to control. In such economies, a change in export receipts or capital flows quickly affects demand and then imports, and since the nominal exchange rate cannot be changed, the foreign sector can stay roughly

Table 10.1
Index of Competitor-Weighted Exchange Rates, 1980-1986 (1980=100)

Sugar		_Citrus_		_Cocoa_	
Dominican Republic	78	Jamaica	88	Dominican Republic	104
Barbados	170	Belize	147	Trinidad & Tobago	167
Guyana	176				
Belize	154				

Coffee		_Beef_	
Dominican Republic	89	Dominican Republic	102
Jamaica	89	Belize	172
Haiti	177	Guyana	200

Source: World Bank estimates based on IMF data, 1988.

in equilibrium only by adjusting factor and product prices, often through adjustments in economic activity. For example, a major price fall (or rise) of an export product could direct economic activity away from (or toward) production of that product, thus smoothing out, over time, the short-term effect on wages and profits.

Mismanagement had postponed the natural tendency toward adjustment, and this has caused a lag in adjusting the real exchange rate over time. This, accompanied with lax demand management, has the effect of discriminating against exports and the country becomes uncompetitive.

One of the results that stems from this paper is that the Caribbean countries were not able to develop new markets, or to diversify and promote their exports in the 1980s, as fully as they could, because of their exchange rate policy. Since all Caribbean countries under study peg their currency to the U.S. dollar, they experienced, along with the dollar, a real appreciation during the early 1980s against virtually all their export markets. This reduced their competitiveness by about 20 to 30 percent, not only in their export markets, but also compared to their competitors. Only the Dominican Republic and Jamaica undertook real devaluations, and then only when their balance of payments was unsustainable. The rapid growth of their manufactured exports after their devaluation confirms the key role exchange rates play in export promotion.

In Barbados, for example, the present cost of the major crop, sugar, is much higher than the world market price (*World Bank, Barbados*, 1988). Barbados' wage costs are among the highest in the Caribbean region and they have been increasing at a rate higher than the rate of inflation. At the same time there are indications that productivity has not matched this increase. The Economist Intelligence Unit (1990) suggests that there is a need for a wage and salary freeze over the next few years in conjunction with an active exchange rate policy. Despite exchange rate adjustments in many Caribbean countries, the Barbadian dollar has been pegged against the U.S. dollar at the rate of BD $ 1.00 = US $ 0.50 since 1975, which caused the BD to appreciate relative to the 1980 base along with the U.S. dollar until the year 1987. An active exchange rate policy should receive more consideration to impose competitiveness.

By contrast the Dominican Republic has two exchange markets. The official exchange rate is pegged to the U.S. dollar.

There is also a "parallel" exchange market (which is tolerated), and this market is supplied by foreign change receipts that are not surrendered at the official exchange rate. The devaluation of its currency to about the 1980 level by 1987 has caused manufactured exports to grow rapidly.

Because of the high degree of market concentration for its merchandise exports and in the source of its tourists, Jamaica is highly sensitive to general economic conditions and to relative exchange rates in its two principal markets   (the United States and the United Kingdom).   Therefore, exchange rate management underwent several modifications. Devaluation of the Jamaican dollar in the 1980s, due to the U.S. dollar appreciation, caused Jamaica's manufactured exports to grow faster than the other Caribbean countries average (*World Bank, Barbados*, 1988).

It is difficult to establish general appropriate economic policies which would be relevant to all countries in the study. Nevertheless, the problems and the constraints are common enough to permit at least a few broad conclusions in regard to exchange rate policies. It is important to declare that there is a need for a sensible financial management policy. If the Caribbean countries wish to improve their long-run growth prospects, they need to capture a good export share in world markets.   Moreover, the choice of export activities poses the question of the extent to which it is desirable to diversify exports both in terms of products and of markets.   More diversification would tend to shield the economy from price and quantity fluctuations, but this has to be balanced against the economies of scale in production, acquisition of technology, and overseas marketing.

Worker productivity must be increased because a decline would not only be inconsistent with fixed exchange rates and wages, it would be even more inconsistent with wage increases. Finally, there is much more effort required of the Caribbean countries themselves. More crucial to any export promotion success is export competitiveness. The Caribbean countries have not used exchange rates effectively until they were forced to. Clearly, more prudent demand management, a more flexible approach to nominal exchange rate adjustments, or both would favor export growth.

11

CARIBBEAN MIGRATION IN A GLOBAL ECONOMY

Ransford W. Palmer

In the 1980s, the centerpiece of U.S. policy toward the Caribbean was the Caribbean Basin Initiative (CBI), which provided duty-free access to a range of imports from the Caribbean. One of the objectives of this policy was to reduce the amount of legal and illegal migration from the region to the United States. The policy was based on the premise that greater access to U.S. markets by Caribbean countries would stimulate the economic development of the region, which would in turn ensure political stability and reduce the propensity of Caribbean people to migrate to the United States. The logic of this premise sounded eminently sensible because Caribbean migration to the United States is primarily driven by economics.

For this policy to have worked, however, it would have had to do more than create jobs; it would have had to reduce the disparity in wages and living standards between the region and the United States. While the creation of jobs in the Caribbean is a necessary condition for reducing the disparity in living standards, it is not a sufficient condition, simply because living standards in the United States and other destination countries are not static. To reduce this disparity, the rate of economic growth in the Caribbean would have had to outstrip those of the destination countries by a wide margin and the distribution of the gains from that growth would have had to be widely distributed throughout the population. The fact is that since 1983 when the CBI was inaugurated, living standards in the Caribbean

have generally declined because of stagnant or negative economic
growth.

The main argument of this chapter is that, even if U.S. policy
had succeeded in stimulating economic growth and reducing the
region's high unemployment rate, it would not have succeeded in
reducing the propensity to migrate in any significant way because of
a combination of factors: the historical perception by Caribbean
workers of their labor market as global; the monopsonistic structure of
domestic labor markets; the particular nature of Caribbean migration;
and the demand for Caribbean workers in a changing U.S. economy.

THE EVOLUTION OF THE PERCEPTION OF
A GLOBAL LABOR MARKET

The slave trade brought Africans to the Caribbean to work in
the sugar cane fields. When slavery was abolished, the colonial
planters imported indentured servants from India and China to replace
freed slaves on the plantation. While the availability of cheap labor
was the lifeblood of the sugar economies, it stifled any incentive on the
part of the planters to modernize their investment by adopting new
technology. As a consequence, Emancipation and the demise of
mercantilism in the latter half of the 19th century left the Caribbean
sugar economies unprepared to compete with the rest of the world.
They were, therefore, unable to provide an adequate livelihood for their
freed labor force. It took U.S. investment in Central America, Cuba,
and Panama to absorb the surplus of unskilled workers in the English
Caribbean. Thus, from Emancipation to World War II, migration from
the Caribbean had overwhelmingly been to countries where foreign
investment generated a demand for low-skilled workers.

After World War II, migration shifted to the labor-short
United Kingdom where thousands of West Indians entered the country
as British citizens to fill low-skill jobs. When Britain closed its doors
to West Indian immigration in 1962, migration shifted to the United
States, stimulated by the liberalization of U.S. immigration policy
under the Immigration and Nationality Act of 1965.

The history of Caribbean migration strongly suggests that the
workers of the region were forced to develop a global perspective on
work. Throughout their history they have worked in industries that

have been global in nature, beginning with sugar, and later tourism, petroleum, and bauxite. As workers in global industries, their vulnerability to global developments has made them particularly sensitive to world market signals. Thus, given their historic perception of their labor market as global, they are always ready to respond to better opportunities elsewhere, even in countries where their language is not spoken. Only the restrictive immigration policies of the destination countries have frustrated their mobility.

THE NATURE OF CARIBBEAN MIGRATION

The change in the nature of Caribbean migration over the past one hundred years has given migration a momentum of its own. Up to World War II, Caribbean migration was temporary in character and was primarily a migration of workers as individuals. Since World War II, migration has become overwhelmingly a movement not just of individual workers but of entire families who seek permanent settlement in their destination countries. This movement of entire households has been encouraged by the family unification feature of U.S. immigration policy. Thus, while U.S. economic policy sought to reduce the propensity of Caribbean people to migrate, U.S. immigration policy encouraged the unification of Caribbean families in the United States. The initial disintegration and ultimate reunification of the Caribbean family through migration may be described as a circular process in which monetary remittances from the destination country play a crucial role.

The immigration household seldom moves as a complete unit. The pattern has been for one adult member to migrate first. Upon employment, the immigrant remits funds to the rest of the household in the country of origin. These remittances help to finance the day-to-day living of those who remain behind as well as their reunification with the new immigrant household abroad. Thus the pattern of contemporary household migration might be described as circular with remittances providing the link which facilitates reunification. As long as some members of the household remain behind, remittances will continue to flow. When the household is completely reunited abroad, this flow will cease, or at least diminish, as the circle of migration is closed. The flow of remittances, then, indicates that household reunification is not complete. Because remittances bring with them the powerful message that things are better abroad, they tend to predispose the recipients to migrate, even if these recipients are not immediate members of the migrating household. Thus, what appears to be a smooth linear flow of people from the Caribbean to the United States over time, upon closer examination, is in fact a set of incomplete circles in various stages of closing, with remittances forming a critical arc. The closing is facilitated by U.S. immigration policy which gives preferential treatment to close relatives.

The mobility of Caribbean households depends to a large extent on its composition. A study of family migration decisions in the United States by Jacob Mincer offers some insights into the international mobility of Caribbean households. Mincer concludes that "Married persons are less likely to move than singles, and the mobility of separated and divorced partners is by far the highest. The mobility of singles is dampened by the fact that many of them are tied to families headed by parents or other close relatives" (1978, 771). Mincer points out that "Since gains and losses from migration are mainly attributable to job mobility, two earner families are more likely to be deterred than single earner families. Single earners in husband and wife families are almost always men, so it is families with working wives whose migration is most likely to be inhibited" (770). It would appear, therefore, that the most mobile households are those headed by single, separated or divorced persons and those with one earner married couple families. In the Caribbean context, the migration of single, separated, or divorced persons fits into the circular migration process when they leave their children behind and send for them later. The same is true for married couple families when the wife and children subsequently join the husband who migrated.

There is a high share of women among Caribbean immigrants. And there is a high probability that most of the women who leave their children behind are single parents. This is based on the fact that the share of children born out of wedlock is extremely high.[1] The mobility of these women with children is facilitated by the extended family, typically an aunt or a maternal grandparent who often takes care of the children until they are sent for. Although in a married couple family the migration decision is usually made by the husband, quite often the decision is made by the wife for whom there are better opportunities for employment abroad. In this case, reunification of the household abroad will depend upon the perceived ease with which the husband may find a job comparable to his current job. Aubrey Bonnett has observed that, in some instances, the reunification does not work because the new economic and social independence achieved by the wife clashes with the traditional expectation of the husband (1990). Given the fact that in Caribbean households there is a disproportionate share of single parents and common law arrangements and that in married couple households the husband as the only earner is still the norm, it is reasonable to conclude that these households tend to have an unusual degree of mobility and that this mobility is reflected in the high propensity to migrate from the region.

Migration begins when a member of the household makes the decision to enhance the lifetime income of the household. This decision is typically based upon the knowledge of employment opportunities abroad gathered from relatives and friends who have migrated, from published sources, or from potential employers. The decision is usually motivated by the wide disparity between earnings at home and earnings abroad as well as by the limited employment choices at home. The limited employment choices and lower level of earnings are themselves determined by the small size and narrow production base of the home economy.

Development strategy in the Caribbean has naturally tended to promote labor-intensive industries to absorb the excess supply of workers. Because labor productivity in these industries is generally low, wage rates tend to be low relative to those in industrial countries where workers work with more and better capital equipment. The problem of worker productivity in the Caribbean is complicated by the fact that, because many workers work in export industries, the value of their marginal product (the measure of worker productivity) is influenced by fluctuations in the price of exports which are dominated by commodities. Thus the measure of labor productivity in a small, export-dependent economy may be unrelated to the amount of capital each worker works with since gains in output per worker may be offset by lower prices. This element of unpredictability becomes part of a complex of factors which influence the decision of those Caribbean workers who seek to maximize their household incomes abroad.

THE MONOPSONISTIC STRUCTURE OF
CARIBBEAN LABOR MARKETS

While differences in labor productivity are the fundamental cause of disparity in wage rates between origin and destination countries, the extent of this disparity is also affected by the competitive structure of the domestic labor market. Normally, a shortage of labor in certain sectors or occupational groups would be expected to push wage rates up. But structural obstacles can prevent this adjustment. Where labor markets are monopsonistic, the extent of this adjustment may be limited, even when labor unions are strong. Caribbean labor markets tend to be monopsonistic in structure in the sense that a large share of the wage labor force is employed by relatively few employers, including the government. Theory tells us that a monopsonistic employer will pay a wage less than what he would pay if he had to compete with other employers for the same workers. When wage rates do not fully reflect the shortage of labor, workers with a global perspective on work are likely to seek out more competitive labor markets abroad, creating the phenomenon of the migration of employed workers. The shortage of skilled labor in certain sectors of the Caribbean economy is accompanied by a surplus in others. The presence of this pool of unemployed workers keeps wage rates down, thereby restricting the lifetime income of each employed worker. Thus, migration from the Caribbean may result from both a shortage and a surplus of labor.

THE DEMAND FOR CARIBBEAN LABOR
IN THE UNITED STATES

The majority of the Caribbean immigrants in the United States work in the rapidly expanding service sector. Because their greatest concentration is in the state of New York and because a large portion of them are employed in health and private household services, it is instructive to examine the future trend of employment in those occupations in the state. The Bureau of Economic Analysis of the U.S. Department of Commerce has projected that between 1988 and 2040, employment and average earnings (in 1982 dollars) in health services in the state of New York will increase by 15.2 percent and 64.6

percent, respectively (See Table 11.1). The employment of private household workers, however, will decline by 27.8 percent. Over this period, the average earnings of the health service worker are expected to grow to almost four times that of the private household worker. The fastest growth in service employment will occur in business, health, and legal services. These projections suggest that even if the demand for Caribbean women for private household work dries up, there will continue to be a strong demand for Caribbean health professionals and technicians.

The 1990 Immigration and Nationality Act, which became effective in 1992, will increase the annual number of visas issued for those with needed professional skills, while reducing the number available to low-skilled immigrants from 18,000 to 10,000. It has been suggested that the reduction in the number of visas for low-skilled immigrants will generate what has been described as the "nanny problem," that is, the shortage of private household workers (Vobejda, 1990, A4). Employers in other labor-intensive industries such as hotels, restaurants, and poultry processing also worry about the potential shortage of low-skilled labor (A4). However, this does not necessarily mean that the inflow of low-skilled labor will decline. Of the overall annual limit of 700,000 immigrant visas set by the 1990 immigration law, up to 480,000 will be made available to the families of U.S. citizens and permanent residents. This means that the United States will continue to receive large inflows of immigrants from countries that have been major sources of immigrants since 1965 as families are reunited. And since a large share of these family members will be spouses and dependents who generally have low skills, the flow of low-skilled immigrants will continue through the family reunification provisions of the law. Barry Chiswick has argued that more than half of the 54,000 visas available for professional and skilled workers prior to the 1990 immigration law went to spouses and dependent children of applicants who are "generally lesser-skilled individuals" (Chiswick, 1990, D3). Further, he points out, "the sixth preference for 'skilled workers and other workers in labor shortage' is a vehicle for the entry of cooks, baby sitters, and other low-skilled workers. About half of the recipients of sixth preference visas in 1989 (excluding spouses and children) were non-professional service occupations" (D3). The point of all this is that a disproportionate share

Table 11.1
Projected Growth of Income and Employment in Selected Services, New York State, 1980-2040

Type of Service	1988			2040			% Change		
	Total Earnings ($ mil./1982)	Employment (000)	Average Earnings	Total Earnings ($ mil./1982)	Employment (000)	Total Earnings	Employment	Average Earnings
All Services	60,075.0	3,026.8	19,848	113,724.1	3,505.8	32,439	15.8	63.4
Private Household	740.0	119.5	6,192	812.7	86.2	9,428	-27.8	52.3
Business	14,464.7	721.7	20,042	24,416.9	977.0	24,992	35.4	24.7
Health	15,458.7	696.3	22,201	29,304.3	801.8	36,548	15.2	64.6
Legal	7,366.4	148.9	49,472	15,888.9	181.1	87,735	21.6	77.3
Educational	3,642.0	256.8	14,182	6,145.7	274.2	22,413	6.8	58.0
Miscellaneous Professional	6,868.1	197.0	34,863	12,223.6	213.0	57,388	8.1	64.6

Source: U.S. Department of Commerce, Bureau of Economic Analysis, BEA Regional Projections to 2040 (Washington, D.C.: U.S. Government Printing Office, 1990).

of low-skilled immigrants enter the United States under the preference for professional and skilled workers.

Despite the shift toward high technology production, the U.S. Department of Labor points out that the country's demand for low-skilled workers will continue to be substantial: "Although the overall pattern of job growth is weighted toward higher skilled occupations, very large numbers of jobs will be created in some medium-to-low-skilled fields" (Hudson Institute, 1987, 99). Indeed in absolute numbers, the biggest job creation categories will be in service occupations, administrative support, and marketing and sales, which together account for half of the net new jobs that will be created. In the service category, the largest groups are cooks, nursing aides, waiters, and janitors. Among administrative support jobs, secretaries, clerks, and computer operators predominate. In marketing and sales, most of the new slots will be for cashiers. With the exception of computer operators, most of these large categories will require only modest level of skills" (99). The great majority of Caribbean immigrants in the United States fill jobs in the rapidly expanding service sector. In one sense, these immigrants provide a cost-effective way of filling these jobs with a minimum of social investment in their education.

SOME CONCLUSIONS

While job creation in the Caribbean is a necessary condition for slowing down legal and illegal migration from the Caribbean to the United States, it is not a sufficient condition. Job creation can restrain migration only if it significantly reduces the disparity in living standards. The migration history of Caribbean workers suggests that they take a global view of work and their employment in global industries has made them sensitive to world market signals. The labor market distortions at home combined with a rapidly growing service sector in the United States and a U.S. immigration policy that encourages family reunification have created a migration momentum that is difficult to slow down.

NOTE

1.   Department of Statistics, *Demographic Statistics* (Kingston, Jamaica: The Government Printer, 1979).

V

CONCLUSION

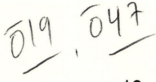

12

EXTERNAL LINKAGES AND GROWTH IN SMALL ECONOMIES

David L. McKee

Although there are as many as eighty Third World jurisdictions with populations in the ten million range or less, the developmental problems of small economies have not received the general attention that appears to be warranted. Until recent advances in transportation and communication, many smaller nations had little reason to be optimistic about their prospects for an improved material status. The smallness of their domestic markets served as a brake on the types of activities which have created both employment and profit opportunities elsewhere and hence, economic expansion.

Prescriptions for import substitution seem hardly capable of being applied successfully in such economies. Thus a wide variety of manufactured goods, which are taken for granted in wealthier nations, have to be imported if they are to be available. If such imports are essential for improving living standards and for growth and development, policymakers have choices to make with respect to what degree of involvement with external economic forces seems prudent or appropriate in keeping with domestic goals or needs. A policy which places severe restrictions on imports and external economic linkages may render even modest developmental objectives unobtainable. At the other end of the continuum a policy which encourages any or all foreign linkages indiscriminately may render reasonable domestic developmental goals impractical in the face of external pressures. Indeed these external pressures may result in adjustments in domestic economies in keeping with the needs of foreign elements in ways which may not be in harmony with the interests of the economies concerned.

The logic of what has been stated here is not intended as a platform to support a restatement of the dependency argument, which most development specialists have encountered. There is no question that there are risks involved for small nations with respect to how they choose to relate to the world economy, larger more powerful nations, and international business operations. The choice for small nations is hardly between involvement or non involvement with the world at large. Instead they must review the types of involvement which may be open to them in terms of their domestic needs and objectives.

For most small Third World jurisdictions a major economic impetus behind their involvement in the world economy comes from decisions to import goods and services which cannot be provided domestically. In the normal course of events nations seek to cover the costs of imports by exporting in turn. In many smaller Third World economies the necessities of foreign trade force difficult decisions on those concerned with domestic development. Such decisions may include a reordering of domestic priorities to include an infrastructure conducive to foreign trade at some cost measured in terms of local needs. They may also include the hosting of foreign-owned production facilities linked to world markets. For small nations who have the options of involving themselves in the world economy a balance must be struck between very real benefits from that involvement and what must be foregone to acquire such benefits. Successful involvement should insure that foreign linkages reinforce domestic developmental goals.

Many small independent nations were first involved with the external world as suppliers of primary products. Although some are still heavily committed to such export activity, it has been becoming increasingly evident throughout this century that primary commodities, notably agricultural products, cannot encourage or sustain the type of economic progress that they are seeking. Aside from the well-known difficulties which agriculture has had with the terms of trade (Nurkse, 1967), economies of scale, in the handling of export crops by larger supplier nations, have made the relatively modest quantities which small nations can supply less attractive to international agribusiness interests. Despite the fact that some needed foreign exchange can be earned through the export of agricultural commodities, redirecting agricultural activity to meet domestic needs appears to be a more beneficial course of action in many cases (McKee and Tisdell, 1990). While providing ongoing employment that practice should reduce the level of food imports, thus assisting in a different way with the balance of trade.

If agriculture and other primary sectors seem unable to provide the foreign exchange that most small countries require, other means must be devised if they are to be able to meet the necessity of paying for essential imports. The gravity of the situation can be seen in Yosra A. Amara's observation (Chapter 2) that "International trade plays a more important role in small countries' economies than in larger ones." Since industrialization is difficult in such small markets, she suggests that the only workable development strategy for small nations with limited natural resources is one of creating export-oriented industries or services. Since she sees many difficulties associated with developing effective manufacturing activities, whether aimed at domestic or export markets, she suggests that services may hold the answer. More specifically she recommends export-oriented services.

Amara sees in services activities which do not have the obvious major disadvantages that are prevalent in agriculture and manufacturing. Because of this, she suggests economies may be able to move directly into services from agriculture without an intermediate stop in manufacturing. She sees services for export as a vehicle for assisting with trade balances while at the same time promoting domestic employment opportunities. The logic of her argument speaks for itself. Small nations where services for export can be encouraged have the potential for improving their development prospects. The specifics must be worked out on a case-by-case basis. Some nations are better positioned and better suited in other ways for the supplying of export services and some may find such pursuits impractical.

Various services have emerged in recent years as important components of the international economy. Transportation and communications services are a prime example. In a very real sense it has been those service groups which have improved international linkages. Certainly it has been those linkages which have given smaller economies broader opportunities to participate internationally. A prime example of the new opportunities rests with international tourism. This of course is a service industry which has improved international linkages as one of its primary causal elements. Amara suggests that technical progress has also encouraged the decentralization of other types of service activities, data processing, for example, which can now be undertaken in small Third World nations.

It seems obvious that all small Third World nations may not share equal opportunities with respect to strengthening their economies through the addition of export oriented services. For example, the small economies in the Caribbean Basin have been able to develop major tourist facilities due to their easy access to a large customer base. No one would suggest that all small Third World jurisdictions can or even should attempt to duplicate what has been done in the Caribbean. International services are hardly a universal growth hormone which can simply be ingested by any or all jurisdictions wishing to expand.

In her second contribution to this volume (Chapter 3), Amara investigates service roles in a selection of small Caribbean jurisdictions. With the exception of Barbados, and perhaps Antigua and Barbuda, the economies which she selected are hardly among those most visible in the region with respect to international service linkages. Nonetheless, she found the service sector in the selected nations to be "more prominent and central than is commonly believed." She found that services "explained large portions of the variability in economic performance" and that the value added by services was strongly related to economic growth. Persuaded by her findings, she recommends serious attention to export services on the part of policymakers concerned with growth and development. Although general guarantees of successful development based on services are hardly warranted, it would seem that small Third World jurisdictions where such service development seems feasible should certainly investigate that option.

In a further attempt to show how foreign linkages impact growth and development in small Third World nations, Ransford Palmer investigates the impact of the instability of export earnings on growth in Jamaica from 1957 to 1986 (Chapter 4). Among his findings is the fact that "services (mainly tourism) and aluminum exports had the greatest impact on the growth of total export earnings." Unfortunately, he found that their contribution to the instability of export earnings exceeded what they contributed to the growth of those earnings. Thus Palmer shows evidence of a major risk which some small economies may encounter as they become involved with exports.

He suggests that, as economic growth becomes more dependent on the exports which he cited, it is likely to be characterized by a greater degree of instability. This of course is one of the risks involved in tourism as a vehicle for development.

Palmer found the period prior to 1973 to be characterized by greater earnings from commodity exports and growth in tourism. These circumstances served as stimuli for capital inflows and thus growth. The 1970s were a period of decline which was characterized by a worsening balance-of-payments situation. A revival of tourism in the 1980s was offset by declining commodity exports, which caused Palmer to raise a question as to "whether tourism can be the engine of growth in the same way that commodities were in the 1960's." He labels tourism as an even more volatile sector than commodity exports, yet acknowledges that the world demand for tourism is rising more rapidly than that for primary products. These observations lead Palmer to conclude that Jamaica must opt for a share in the expansion of tourism while at the same time diversifying its exports as a buffer against the inherent instability of tourism.

Speaking of services in general, Palmer found that the change in the composition of exports toward service dominance has been accompanied by higher instability in export earnings. He attributes this to the instability of both world prices and the exchange rate. Thus it appears that small economies trading services in world markets introduce instabilities to their domestic operations because of external fluctuations which are beyond their control. In the Jamaican case, Palmer would hardly seek a remedy through limiting exports. If imports are to be funded it seems as though small nations must be prepared for a certain amount of instability in their economies caused by export demand.

Implicit in the question raised by Charles Byles, "Can Caribbean Firms Compete Globally?" (Chapter 5), is the assumption that doing so is important. Certainly it would appear to be if such firms are to aid the jurisdictions which house them in securing foreign exchange not to mention ongoing growth and development. Writing about the former British colonies in the Caribbean, Byles addresses various issues internal to the firms themselves. He is critical of conditions in the Caribbean which are only geared to moderate change and suggests that business firms are risk-averse. He sees business firms in the region as characterized by "an entrenched attitude and style of leadership which is counterproductive." Economists might label such behavior as traditional. If this pattern of behavior exists in small economies it may very well interfere with international competitiveness. If cultural or business attitudes in the Caribbean or other small nations elsewhere tend to block or retard success in international ventures, some would suggest that changes in the direction of greater efficiency are indicated if growth and development are to be achieved. Economists and others concerned with development no longer take the potential pain inherent in such adjustments lightly.

Byles cites the minimal level of rivalry among firms in the domestic markets of the Caribbean as a factor in their efficiency and effectiveness. Certainly local markets in small economies can hardly be expected to support a number of competitors supplying a specific good or service for the same reason that import substitution in certain product lines is impossible. A lack of efficiency in firms producing for local markets is hardly a suitable base for launching the export of their products.

As Byles suggested, "challenges facing many firms come not from competitors but from economic conditions...government policies...and work attitudes and behavior...and the general difficulty with getting even the simplest task done." Any of these factors may interfere with the ability of small economies to compete internationally. Together they represent what Schumpeter might have called the business climate. In specific jurisdictions such factors must be addressed by the policymakers if successful linkages with the international economy are to be forged.

Byles suggests that firms seem willing to merely survive with little concern for the quality of their products or service offerings. In various service pursuits, notably hotels and car rentals, he suggests that firms in Caribbean jurisdictions are at a disadvantage in serving clients from abroad because "they do not fully understand the standards to which these clients are accustomed." Small domestic markets where buyers are only moderately demanding are hardly a good training ground for success with a foreign clientele used to international standards. It is clear that Byles feels that Caribbean firms are not in a very strong position to compete internationally. Of course if his reasoning is to be applied to small economies elsewhere in the world it will have to be reexamined on a case-by-case basis. At the very least he has explored potential pitfalls for development strategies based upon successful competition in world markets.

Further evidence of international involvement can be seen in Chapter 6, which discusses the prospects for the Haitian economy. Aside from having to import finished products, that nation is faced with the necessity of importing substantial quantities of food. Indeed food imports are inching their way toward 20 percent of total imports. The nation's poor economic circumstances make it very difficult to practice significant import substitution. Thus Haiti is faced with the continuing problem of paying for needed imports. Because of its heavy reliance upon imports the nation "finds changes in the international environment impacting nearly every aspect of its economic structure" (Chapter 6). Among small nations which are poor Haiti is hardly alone in this dilemma.

Manufacturing operations in Haiti have not been doing well because of difficulties in obtaining the hard currency needed for imported inputs. Environmental difficulties face the restructuring of agriculture to cover domestic needs. Haiti's prospects may be brighter in certain types of service activity, particularly those of the labor-intensive variety. In pursuit of services which can earn foreign exchange, Haiti may be somewhat disadvantaged with respect to various other Caribbean nations due to literacy levels, not to mention issues related to infrastructure. Service activities such as data processing and other office related services may have potential as does tourism. Attention to service activities with export potential seems indicated if Haiti and perhaps other small nations facing similar circumstances are to improve their balance-of-payments positions and lay the groundwork for economic expansion.

Writing about small island economies, Mary Fish and William D. Gunther suggest that such jurisdictions "may be physically close to more developed countries but economically distant in terms of their ability to service international trade." In such economies they suggest that tourism is frequently of considerable economic importance and is often the primary export earner. They are quite correct in suggesting that such economies, despite rather heavy involvement in tourism, are still relatively small participants in a large international industry. Thus dependence upon tourism means in turn a dependence upon events well beyond the control of any small jurisdiction.

Fish and Gunther see tourism as especially sensitive to international terrorism and acts of violence. They point to recent events involving Iraq and Kuwait as having had a dramatic negative impact on international travel. Beyond such events they point out that any form of political upheaval in prospective tourist destinations will depress the industry in such locations. They suggest that the threat of violence in one jurisdiction may depress tourism in other small nations in a region, citing problems in Jamaica as a depressant to tourism elsewhere in the Caribbean in the early 1980s. Certainly such problems point to the vulnerability of small economies to events beyond their boundaries. Despite the risks many small nations are hardly able to forego their involvement in tourism. Nonetheless, a broadening of the economic base seems indicated where possible.

A subset of international tourism which small Third World nations have even less control over is the business of cruise vacations. Certainly the issues alluded to by Fish and Gunther apply to this segment of the leisure travel industry as well. Not only has the industry had direct experience with terrorism, its customer base is impacted by the threat of violence in ways similar to the tourist industry in general. Beyond violence and terrorism the industry is influenced by world economic conditions. For instance, hard economic times in the United States and Canada impact cruise tourism in the Caribbean. Obviously, some Third World destinations do not have the option of hosting cruise ships but those who do are involving themselves in an industry, the fortunes of which may be well beyond their control. Caution should be exercised in adjusting domestic priorities too far to accommodate cruise ships. This is most important in the smallest and poorest potential host jurisdictions.

As stated earlier (Chapter 8), it would appear that cruise visitors provide both employment and profit opportunities for host nations. To some extent these benefits are attainable; however, it should be realized that the visiting ships are actually competing with their hosts for tourist dollars. "To the extent that they are successful the positive impacts of cruise ships upon host ports and their economies will be reduced." The bottom line for potential host jurisdictions must be some obvious developmental gain.

Cruise visits are a way in which potential host nations can display themselves to masses of visitors without the major investments in hotels and facilities which land-based tourism involves. In nations wishing to develop more permanent links to the tourist industry this may be a plus. However, such jurisdictions must be cognizant of the costs of an infrastructure to support cruise ships as well as the potential gains from hosting them. A major short-run benefit from hosting cruise ships would be an increase in on-shore spending on the part of passengers. To date evidence from various destinations suggests rather modest per capita outlays from passengers.

Although cruise lines advertise exotic destinations, they are becoming increasingly adept at keeping passengers on board. This is done by increasing their shopping and entertainment facilities and by broadening on-board experiences in other ways. Reducing the number of ports of call has the same effect as does the practice of securing more remote anchorages where passengers can be given opportunities for water recreation off deserted beaches where they add neither jobs nor profits to host economies. The trend toward larger ships may preclude visits to smaller host nations barring extraordinary outlays on infrastructure. In short, cruise tourism is an example of an industry where the firms are in a strong position in their relations with host jurisdictions. Those jurisdictions should take care in placing too much reliance upon cruise tourism.

In her final contribution to the current volume, Amara turns her attention to exchange rates and financial policy as factors impacting the prospects of small developing countries. Specifically, she discusses the economic role of an efficient exchange rate regime and sound financial policy against a backdrop of data for a selection of Caribbean jurisdictions. Returning to a theme which was introduced earlier (Chapter 2), she suggests that in small nations, such as those selected, the international market is more important than in larger jurisdictions with wider operations. She suggests that "as growth proceeds, in very small countries there is every indication that the degree of openness will become even greater" (Chapter 10).

Some nations may attempt to buy a certain amount of stability in their external relationships by pegging their currencies to that of their principal trading partner. Amara suggests that such pegging cannot entirely insulate an economy. In small nations such as those in the Caribbean she feels that this is due to the high level of external trade as compared to domestic production. She suggests that a country choosing fixed over flexible exchange rates gives up its right to have control over the value of its currency, nor will it be able to control its rate of inflation.

Amara points out that small nations which peg their currencies to that of one major country tie their price levels to that of the chosen country and leave themselves invariant to changes among "key-currency values and price levels in the rest of the world." No pegging to a single currency will insulate the domestic price level from fluctuations among key currencies. As she explains, pegging to a single currency will result in variations in the effective exchange rate of the nations concerned. The variations in question stem from fluctuations among key currencies and are not related to the balance-of-payments position of the jurisdiction in question. Amara suggests that a nation can reduce its loss of control over its effective exchange rate by pegging to a weighted average of key currencies. If such a nation wishes to maintain domestic prices in line with the "world" price level, the weights chosen, she feels, should correspond to those of each major country contributing to such a price level. It seems clear that the necessity for trading in world markets forces complicated financial choices upon small economies. Indeed, keeping the trade situation in reasonable balance may dictate financial choices which will have unavoidable impacts in the domestic sectors of such economies.

In a second contribution to this volume, Ransford Palmer examines the tendency for workers in the Caribbean to be willing to enter labor markets beyond their shores. Until relatively recently it seems as though Caribbean jurisdictions, particularly those which were former British colonies, had been relying upon out-migration as a means of controlling tendencies toward overpopulation. This phenomenon was certainly in evidence earlier in this century. The exporting of surplus population is yet another way in which small nations form linkages with the world economy and/or other nations. Aside from keeping population in check, out-migration from small Third World nations results in remittances which make substantial contributions to the economies in question.

Palmer's concerns are not coextensive with what has been stated above. His discussion is set against the backdrop of the Caribbean Basin Initiative, which highlighted U.S. policy toward the Caribbean during the 1980s. Palmer saw that policy as based upon the supposition that broad access to markets in the United States would stimulate development in the Caribbean nations concerned, thus ensuring political stability and cutting back on the tendency for Caribbean people to emigrate. Palmer feels that, regardless of whether or not the policy was successful, migration would continue for reasons which the policy could not influence. He suggests that Caribbean workers see their labor market as global. Beyond that "the monopsonistic structure of domestic markets; the tendency for entire households to migrate; the support for family unification in U.S. immigration policy; and the demand for service workers in a changing U.S. economy" all contribute to pressures to migrate.

Palmer sees the reduction in the interest in migration among workers in the Caribbean as dependent upon the reduction in international disparities in living standards through economic growth. With the emergence of large trading blocks he seems optimistic that the small nations of the Caribbean may be able to improve their positions. Whether a similar optimistic prognosis applies in other small Third World settings is destination specific. Small nations that are isolated or poorly linked to the international economy may have limited growth prospects. Such nations may have tendencies toward overpopulation and thus may see out-migration as advantageous where feasible. Of course out-migration forms international linkages which may prove helpful, but it may also embrace a drain of workers with needed skills. Small economies would do well to consider the potential impact of such population adjustments.

The present volume does not pretend to have exhausted the ways in which small Third World economies are becoming linked to the international economy. However, it should suggest the broad scope that such linkages may take. It may also lend support to the thesis that international linkages are inevitable in such small jurisdictions. If that is true, it also supports the need for those concerned with expansion in small economies to pay careful attention to the international sphere.

BIBLIOGRAPHY

Alexander, Sidney S. (1952). "Effect of Devaluation on a Trade Balance." *Staff Papers*, Vol. 2, April, 263-78.

Archer, E. (1984). "Estimating the Relationship Between Tourism and Economic Growth in Barbados." *Journal of Travel Research*, Vol. 22, no. 4, 8-12.

Barry, Tom, Beth Wood, and Deb Preusch. (1984). *The Other Side of Paradise: Foreign Control in the Caribbean.* New York: Grove Press.

Beckford, George L. (1972). *Persistent Poverty: Underdevelopment in Plantation Economies of the Third World.* London: Oxford University Press.

Beckford, George and Norman Girvan (eds.). (1988). *Development in Suspense.* Kingston, Jamaica: Friedrich Ebert Stiftung in collaboration with the Association of Caribbean Economists.

Berger, P. L. (1984). "Can the Caribbean Learn from East Asia?" *Caribbean Review*, Vol. 13, 7-9, 40-41.

Bernal, R. L. (1984). "Foreign Investment and Development in Jamaica." *InterAmerican Economic Affairs*, Vol. 38, no. 2, 3-21.

Bhaduri, Amit, Anjan Mukherji, and Ramprasad Sengupta. (1982). "Problems of Long-Term Growth: A Theoretical Analysis." In Bimal Jalan (ed.), *Problems and Policies in Small Economies.* New York: St. Martin's Press, 49-68.

Bond, Marian E. (1979). "The World Trade Model: Invisibles." *International Monetary Fund: Staff Papers 2*, June, 257-333.

Bonnett, Aubrey. (1990). "The New Female West Indian Immigrant:
    Dilemmas of Coping in the Host Society." In Ransford W. Palmer
    (ed.), *In Search of a Better Life*. New York: Praeger, 115-138.

Boodhoo, Ken I. (1989). "U.S.-Haitian Relations." *Caribbean Affairs*, Vol. 1,
    no. 4, 49-63.

Brady, John and Richard Widdows. (1988). "The Impact of World Events on
    Travel to Europe during the Summer of 1986." *Journal of Travel
    Research*, Vol. XXVI, no. 3, Winter, 8-10.

Broadwell, Laura. (1986). "Evaluating Terrorism." *Incentive Marketing*, Vol.
    160, no. 2, February, 16-21.

Caribbean Tourism Research and Development Centre. (1988).   *Caribbean
    Tourism Statistical Report 1988*. Christ Church, Barbados, CTRDC.

Centaur Associates, Inc. (1980).   *Analysis of the North American Cruise
    Industry*.   Prepared   for   the   Maritime   Administration,   U.S.
    Department of Commerce, October.

Central Bank of Barbados. (1987).   *Annual Statistical Digest*. Barbados:
    Bridgetown.

Chenery, Hollis and D. B. Keesing. (1979). "The Changing Composition of
    Developing Country Exports." *The World Bank Staff Working Paper
    314*, Washington, D.C.: World Bank.

Chiswick, Barry R. (1990). "Opening the Golden Door." *Washington Post*,
    October 7, D3.

Clark, Colin. (1940).   *The Conditions of Economic Progress*. 3d ed.   New
    York: St. Martin's Press.

Clermont, Charles. (1989).   "Haiti: Adjustment Policies and Development
    Strategies." In Beckford and Girvan (eds.) (1988), *Development in
    Suspense*.   Kingston,   Jamaica: Friedrich   Ebert   Stiftung   in
    collaboration with the Association of Caribbean Economists, 88-99.

CLIA. (1987).   *An Overview of the U.S. Cruise Industry*.   Cruise Lines
    International Association.

Conant, Jeffrey S., Terry Clark, John J. Burnett, and Gail Zank. (1988).
    "Terrorism and Travel: Managing the Unmanageable." *Journal of
    Travel Research*, Vol. XXVI, no. 4, Spring, 16-20.

Connolly, Michael. (1985).   "The Exchange Rate and Monetary and Fiscal
    Problems in Jamaica." In Michael Connolly and John McDermont
    (eds.), *The Economics of the Caribbean*.   New York: Praeger
    Publishers, 237-50.

Crusol, Jean. (1980). *Economies Insulaires de la Caraibe: Aspects Theoriques
    et Pratiques du Development*. Paris: Edition Caribeennes.

Davis, C. G., W. K. Mathis, and M. T. Futa. (1980). "The Determinants of Instability of Agricultural Export Earnings in Sub-Saharan African Economies." *Social and Economic Studies*, Vol. 29, nos. 2 and 3, June/September, 89-106.

Economist Intelligence Unit. (1988). "Guyana, Barbados, Windward & Leeward Islands 1987-88." *Country Profile*. London: The Economist Intelligence Unit, 35-46.

___. (1989-1990). *Guyana, Barbados, Windward & Leeward Islands: Country Profile*. London: The Economist Intelligence Unit.

___. (1990). *Country Profile, Different Issues*. London: The Economist Intelligence Unit.

___. (1990). *Trinidad and Tobago, Guyana, Barbados, Windward & Leeward Islands: Country Report 2*. London: The Economist Intelligence Unit.

Fisher, Allan G. B. (1939). *Economic Self Sufficiency*. New York: Farrar and Rinehart, Inc.

___. (1939). "Production, Primary, Secondary and Tertiary." *Economic Record*, 15, June, 24-38.

Foster, Douglas. (1985). *Travel and Tourism Management*. London: MacMillan.

Frankel, Jeffrey A. (1985). Six Possible Meanings of "Overvaluation." *The 1981-1985 Dollar*. Princeton, New Jersey: Princeton University Press.

Friedman, Milton and Allan Meltzer. (1973). "How Well Are Fluctuating Exchange Rates Working?" *The Subcommittee on International Economics of the Joint Economic Committee: Congress of the United States*, 20, 21, 26, and 27 June, 126ff.

Fuchs, Victor R. (1964). *Productivity Trends in the Goods and Service Sectors, 1929-61: A Preliminary Survey*. New York: Columbia University Press.

___. (1965). "The Growing Importance of the Service Industries." *Journal of Business of the University of Chicago*, Vol. 38, 344-73.

___. (1968). *The Service Economy*. New York: Columbia University Press.

Gemmell, Norman. (1982). "Economic Development and Structural Change: The Role of the Service Sector." *The Journal of Development Studies*, Vol. 19, 37-66.

Ghali, M. A. (1976). "Tourism and Economic Growth: An Empirical Study." *Economic Development and Cultural Change*, Vol. 24, April, 527-38.

Gorman, Christine. (1991). "From Warfare to Fare Wars." *Time*, Vol. 137, no. 14, April 8, 49-50.

Harrigan, Norwell. (1974). "The Legacy of Caribbean History and Tourism." *Annals of Tourism Research*, Vol. 2, no. 1, 13-25.

Hofstede, G. (1980a). *Culture's Consequences.* (Abridged Edition). Beverly Hills, California: Sage Publications.

___. (1980b). "Motivation, Leadership and Organization: Do American Theories Apply Abroad?" *Organizational Dynamics*, Summer, 42-63.

Holloway, J. Christopher. (1986). *The Business of Tourism.* 2nd ed. London: Pitman.

Hudson Institute. (1987). *Workforce 2000: Work and Workers for the 21st Century* (Indianapolis, Indiana: Hudson Institute): 99.

Hurley, John A. (1988). "The Hotels of Rome: Meeting the Marketing Challenge of Terrorism." *The Cornell H.R.A. Quarterly*, May, 71-79.

International Monetary Fund. (1989a). *International Financial Statistics.* Washington, D.C.: International Monetary Fund.

___. (1989b). *Direction of Trade Statistics Yearbook.* Washington, D.C.: International Monetary Fund.

___. (1982 and 1990). *International Financial Statistics.* Washington, D.C.: International Monetary Fund.

Investment Climate Statement Jamaica. (1990). Published by the United States Department of Commerce, International Trade Administration, Washington, D.C., April.

Jalan, Bimal (ed.). (1982). *Problems and Policies in Small Economies.* New York: St. Martin's Press.

Jud, G. D. and W. Krause. (1976). "Evaluating Tourism in Developing Areas: An Exploratory Inquiry." *Journal of Travel Research*, Vol. 15, 1-9.

Katouzian, M. A. (1970). "The Development of the Service Sector: A New Approach." *Oxford Economic Papers*, Vol. 22, November, 362-82.

Kendall, Lane C. (1983). *The Business of Shipping.* 4th ed.   Centreville, Maryland: Cornell Maritime Press.

Krueger, Anne O. (1985). "How to Liberalize a Small Open Economy." In Michael B. Connolly, and John McDermont (eds.), *The Economics of the Caribbean Basin.* New York: Praeger Publishers, 13-23.

Kuznets, Simon. (1965). *Economic Growth and Structure: Selected Essays.* New York: W. W. Norton.

___. (1968). *Toward a Theory of Economic Growth.* New York: W. W. Norton.

___. (1971) *Economic Growth of Nations: Total Output and Production Structure*. Cambridge, Massachusetts: Harvard University Press.

Legarda, Benito. (1984). "Small Island Economies." *Finance and Development*, Vol. 21, no. 2, June, 42-43.

Levitt, T. (1986) *The Marketing Imagination*. (New, Expanded Edition). New York: The Free Press.

Lim, David. (1983). "Instability of Government Revenue and Expenditure in Less Developed Countries." *World Development*, Vol. II, no. 5, May, 447-50.

Lloyd, P. J. and R. M. Sundrum. (1982). "Characteristics of Small Economies." In Bimal Jalan (ed.), *Problems and Policies in Small Economies*. New York: St. Martin's Press, 17-38.

Lundberg, D. E. (1980). *The Tourist Business*. Boston: Cohnors Books.

Mamoozadeh, Abbas and David L. McKee. (1990). "Development Through Tourism: Some Economic and Financial Issues." *Tijdschrift Voor Economic en Management*, Vol. XXXV, no. 2 (avril-juin), 147-57.

Manley, M. (1990). *The Politics of Change* (Rev. ed.). Kingston, Jamaica: Heinemann Publishers (Caribbean) Limited.

Maslow, A. (1970). *Motivation and Personality*. 2nd ed. New York: Harper and Row.

Massel, Benton F. (1964). "Export Concentration and Fluctuations in Export Earnings: A Cross-sectional Analysis." *American Economic Review*, Vol. 54, no. 2, 47-63.

McCallum, B. T. (1970). "Artificial Orthogonalization in Regression Analysis." *Review of Economics and Statistics*, Vol. 52, 110-13.

McGregor, D. (1960). *The Human Side of Enterprise*. New York: McGraw-Hill.

McKee, David L. (1977). "Facteurs extérieurs et infrastructure des pays en voie de développement." *Revue Tiers-Monde*, Vol. 18, no. 70 (avril-juin), 1977, 293-300.

___. (1988). *Growth, Development and the Service Economy in the Third World*. New York: Praeger Publishers.

___. (1991). *Schumpeter and the Political Economy of Change*. New York: Praeger Publishers.

___ and Clem Tisdell. (1990). *Developmental Issues in Small Island Economies*. New York: Praeger Publishers.

McKinnon, Ronald and Donald Mathieson. (1981). "How to Manage a Repressed Economy." *Princeton Essays in International Finance*, 145 (12), Princeton, New Jersey: Princeton University Press.

Meier, Gerald M. (1982). *Problems of a World Monetary Order*. 2d ed., New York: Oxford University Press.

Miles, R. E. and C. C. Snow. (1978). *Organization Strategy, Structure, and Process*. New York: McGraw-Hill.

Miller, Willis H. (1985). "The U.S. Cruise Ship Industry." *Journal of Geography*, Vol. 84, no. 5, September-October.

Mincer, Jacob. (1978). "Family Migration Decisions." *Journal of Political Economy*, Vol. 86, October, 771.

Mintzberg, H. (1973). "Strategy-Making in Three Modes." *California Management Review*, Vol. 15, no. 2, 44-53.

__. (1979). *The Structuring of Organizations*. Englewood Cliffs, New Jersey: Prentice-Hall.

Monroe, T. (1972). *The Politics of Constitutional Decolonization: Jamaica 1944-62*. Institute of Social and Economic Research, University of the West Indies, Kingston, Jamaica.

Murray, David. (1978). "Export Earnings Instability: Price, Quantity, Supply, Demand?" *Economic Development and Cultural Change*, Vol. 27, No. 1, October, 68-69.

Nell, Edward. (1988). *Prosperity and Public Spending: Transformational Growth and the Role of Government*. Boston: Unwin Hyman.

Nicholls, J.A.F., M. Lyn-Cook, and S. Roslow (1990). "A Framework for Effective Export Marketing: The Jamaican Partnership of Public Policy and Private Enterprise." *Journal of Public Policy and Marketing*, Vol. 9, 195-210.

Nurkse, Ragnar. (1967). *Problems of Capital Formation in Underdeveloped Countries and Patterns of Trade and Development*. New York: Oxford University Press.

Oglethorpe, Miles. (1985). "Tourism in a Small Island Economy: The Case of Malta." *Tourism Management*, Vol. 6, no. 1, March, 23-31.

Page, Ken. (1987). "The Future of Cruise Shipping." *Tourism Management*, Vol. 8, no. 2, 166-68.

Palmer, Ransford W. (1979). *Caribbean Dependence on the United States Economy*. New York: Praeger.

Parry, Thomas G. (1973). "The International Firm and National Economic Policy." *Economic Journal*, Vol. 84, no. 332, December, 1201-21.

Porter, M. E. (1985). *Competitive Advantage*. New York: The Free Press.

__. (1990a). *The Competitive Advantage of Nations*. New York: The Free Press.

__. (1990b). "The Competitive Advantage of Nations." *Harvard Business Review*, Vol. 68, no. 2, 73-93.

Portes, Alejandro and Lauren Benton. (1984). "Industrial Development and Labor Absorption: A Reinterpretation." *Population & Development Review*, Vol. 10, no. 4, December, 589-611.

Prebisch, R. (1958). "Commercial Policy in the Underdeveloped Countries." *American Economic Review Papers and Proceeding*, Vol. 49 (May).

Punnett, B. J. (1986). "Motivating Employees in the Caribbean: An Empirical Study in St. Vincent and the Grenadines." *Canadian Journal of Latin American and Caribbean Studies*, 71-82.

Ram, Rati. (1985). "Exports and Growth: Some Additional Evidence." *Economic Development and Cultural Change*, Vol. 33, no. 2, January, 415-22.

__. (1987). "Exports and Economic Growth in Developing Countries: Evidence from Time Series and Cross-section Data." *Economic Development and Cultural Change*, Vol. 36, no. 1, October, 51-72.

Richter, Linda K. and William L. Waugh, Jr. (1986). "Terrorism and Tourism as Logical Companions." *Tourism Management*, Vol. 6, no. 4, December, 230-38.

Riddle, Dorothy I. (1987). "The Role of the Service Sector in Economic Development: Similarities and Differences by Development Category." In Orio Giarini (ed.), *The Emerging Service Economy*. New York: Pergamon Press, 83-104.

Roemer, Michael. (1978). *Fishing for Growth: Export Led Development in Peru 1950-1967*. Cambridge, Mass.: Harvard University Press.

Rosensweig, J. A. (1988). "Elasticities of Substitution in Caribbean Tourism." *Journal of Development Economics*, Vol. 20, no. 1, July, 89-100.

Shelp, Ronald Kent. (1981). *Beyond Industrialization: Ascendancy of the Global Service Economy*. New York: Praeger Publishers.

Singelmann, Joachim. (1978). *From Agriculture to Services: The Transformation of Industrial Employment*. Beverly Hills, California: Sage Publications.

Stigler, George J. (1956). *Trends in Employment in the Service Industries*. Princeton, New Jersey: Princeton University Press.

Suraiya, Jug. (1990). "Trouble in Shangri La." *Far Eastern Economic Review*, May 3.

Teye, Victor B. (1988). "Coups D'Etat and African Tourism: A Study of Ghana." *Annals of Tourism Research*, Vol. 15, no. 3, 329-56.

Theil, Henry. (1961). *Economic Forecasts and Policy*. New York: North Holland.

Thomas, Ian. (1982). "The Industrialization Experience of Small Economies." In Bimal Jalan (ed.), *Problems and Policies in Small Economies*. New York: St. Martin's Press, 103-24.

Vobejda, Barbara. (1990). "Immigration Measure Raises Hopes, Worries." *Washington Post*, November 4, A4.

Wilkinson, P. F. (1987). "Tourism in Small Island Nations: A Fragile Dependence." *Leisure Studies*, Vol. 6, 127-46.

Wilkinson, Paul F. (1989). "Strategies for Tourism in Island Microstates." *Annals of Tourism Research*, Vol. 16, no. 2, 153-77.

Witter, Michael. (1983). "Exchange Rate Policy in Jamaica: A Critical Assessment," *Social and Economic Studies*, Vol. 32, no. 4, December, 1-50.

The World Bank. (1985). *Antigua and Barbuda: Economic Report*. Washington, D.C.: World Bank.

___. (1985). *St. Christopher and Nevis: Economic Report*. Washington, D.C.: World Bank.

___. (1985). *St. Lucia: Economic Performance and Prospects*. Washington, D.C.: World Bank.

___. (1985). *St. Vincent and the Grenadines: Economic Situation and Selected Development Issues*, Washington, D.C.: World Bank.

___. (1988). *Antigua and Barbuda: Updating Economic Note 7115*.

___. (1988). *Barbados: The Need for Economic Policy Adjustment 7184*. Washington, D.C.: Latin America and the Caribbean Regional Office. Washington, D.C.: Latin America and the Caribbean Regional Office.

___. (1988). *Caribbean Countries: Economic Situation, Regional Issues, and Capital Flows*. Washington, D.C.: The International Bank for Reconstruction and Development.

___. (1988). *Caribbean Exports: Preferential Markets and Performance 7202* (May), Washington, D.C.: International Economics Department.

___. (1988). *Caribbean Exports: Preferential Markets and Performance 7207*. Washington, D.C.: Latin America and the Caribbean Regional Office.

___. (1988). *Caribbean Region: Current Situation, Issues and Prospects 7215* (April), Washington, D.C.: Latin America and the Caribbean Regional Office.

___. (1988).   *St. Kitts and Nevis: Diversification and Growth 7171.*
Washington, D.C.: Latin America and the Caribbean Regional
Office.

___. (1988). *St. Lucia Economic Memorandum 7117.* Washington, D.C.: Latin
America and the Caribbean Regional Office.

___. (1988). *St. Vincent and the Grenadines Economic Memorandum 7075.*
Washington, D.C.: Latin America and the Caribbean Regional
Office.

___. (1988). *World Development Report.* Washington, D.C.: Oxford University
Press.

___. (1989). *World Development Report.* Washington, D.C.: Oxford University
Press.

World Trade Organization. (1986). *Yearbook of Tourism Statistics.* Spain.

Worrell, D. (1987). *Small Island Economies: Structure and Performance in
the English-Speaking Caribbean Since 1970.* New York: Praeger.

INDEX

ABOUT THE EDITOR AND CONTRIBUTORS

DAVID L. MCKEE is Professor of Economics at Kent State University. He is a specialist in economic development and regional economics. His research has been widely published in professional journals in the United States and abroad. His recent books include *Schumpeter and the Political Economy of Change*; *Growth, Development, and the Service Economy in the Third World*; *Developmental Issues in Small Island Economies* (coauthored with Clement Tisdell), and *Accounting Services, the International Economy and Third World Development* (coauthored with Don E. Garner).

YOSRA A. AMARA is a recent Ph.D. graduate of Kent State University and a specialist in International Economics. Her research interests include exchange rate issues and developmental problems in small Third World nations.

CHARLES M. BYLES is Assistant Professor of Management at Virginia Commonwealth University where he specializes in Strategic Management and International Management. He is especially knowledgeable on matters concerning the nations of the Caribbean, having had both university and private sector experience in that region.

MARY FISH is Professor of Economics at the University of Alabama where she specializes in Macroeconomics, Economics of Tourism, and Economics of Special Groups. She has been a Fulbright Senior Lecturer at the University of Liberia and a consultant to the Gambian Government. Her work has been widely published in the professional literature.

WILLIAM D. GUNTHER is Associate Dean for Research, Director of the Center for Business and Economic Research, and Professor of Economics at the University of Alabama. He has been Visiting Fulbright Professor at the University of Veracruz, Mexico, and Senior Fulbright Professor at the University of Amazonia, Brazil. He is Executive Director of Omicron Delta Epsilon and a board member of the Institute for Waste Management Studies. His articles have appeared in many professional journals.

ABBAS MAMOOZADEH is Associate Professor of Economics and Finance and Chair of the Department of Economics and Finance at Slippery Rock University. He is knowledgeable in International Finance and Economic Development and has lectured and written on issues involving various Caribbean jurisdictions.

RANSFORD W. PALMER is Graduate Professor of Economics at Howard University. Dr. Palmer has been president of the Caribbean Studies Association, a Brookings Institution Economic Policy Fellow, and a Danforth Associate. A specialist in international trade and development, his books include *Problems of Development in Beautiful Countries: Perspectives on the Caribbean*; *Caribbean Dependence on the United States Economy*; and *The Jamaican Economy*.